TOUCHING GOD

Currents in Comparative Romance Languages and Literatures

Tamara Alvarez-Detrell and Michael G. Paulson
General Editors

Vol. 144

PETER LANG
New York • Washington, D.C./Baltimore • Bern
Frankfurt am Main • Berlin • Brussels • Vienna • Oxford

Beth Kathryn Curran

TOUCHING GOD

The Novels of Georges Bernanos
in the Films of Robert Bresson

PETER LANG
New York • Washington, D.C./Baltimore • Bern
Frankfurt am Main • Berlin • Brussels • Vienna • Oxford

Library of Congress Cataloging-in-Publication Data

Curran, Beth Kathryn.
Touching God: the novels of Georges Bernanos
in the films of Robert Bresson / Beth Kathryn Curran.
p. cm. — (Currents in comparative Romance languages
and literatures; v. 144)
Includes bibliographical references.
1. Bernanos, Georges, 1888–1948—Film and video adaptations.
2. Bernanos, Georges, 1888–1948—Criticism and interpretation. 3. Bresson,
Robert—Criticism and interpretation. I. Title. II. Series.
PQ2603.E5875Z6695   843'.912—dc22   2005025656
ISBN 0-8204-7826-1
ISSN 0893-5963

Bibliographic information published by **Die Deutsche Bibliothek**.
Die Deutsche Bibliothek lists this publication in the "Deutsche
Nationalbibliografie"; detailed bibliographic data is available
on the Internet at http://dnb.ddb.de/.

© 2006 Peter Lang Publishing, Inc., New York
29 Broadway, New York, NY 10006
www.peterlang.com

Printed in Germany

For my parents

TABLE OF CONTENTS

ACKNOWLEDGMENTS

I am indebted to Leonard Swidler and Alan Williams for their invaluable critiques of the manuscript at various stages of its composition.

I am deeply grateful to all the members of my family for their love and emotional support, to my friends for their affection and sense of humor, and to my students for their part in the joy of teaching.

INTRODUCTION

Robert Bresson (1901–1999) is the author of an exceptional yet sparse canon of films. Aside from a short comedy, *Les Affaires publiques* (1934), he made thirteen feature-length films during a cinematic career of forty years: *Les Anges du péché* was released in 1943 and *L'Argent* in 1983. Bresson also planned a life of Saint Ignatius of Loyola and an adaptation of the book of Genesis, but neither was ever made. The filmmaker remains a mysterious figure, as very little is known about his life. He exercised astonishing control over what information was available about him to keep his personal life hidden—even concealing basic details of his biography, such as his date of birth.

What details we do know about Bresson are vague: he began his career as a painter, turned to scriptwriting in the nineteen-thirties, and spent the beginning of World War II in a German prison camp before resuming his cinematic career. Bresson became famous for his insistence on privacy by directing critics' attention away from his life to his films. In 1972, Bresson offered this response to Paul Schrader's book, *Transcendental Style in Film: Ozu, Bresson, Dreyer*: "I have always been very surprised not to recognize myself in the image formed by those who are really interested in me."[1]

Fortunately, we have access to Bresson's own words about his experience as a filmmaker, found in his often quoted *Notes sur le cinématographe*. These aphoristic reflections on the principles and practice of his unique approach to filmmaking mostly date from between 1950 and 1958, with a smaller number from between 1960 and 1974. Bresson's main concern is his rejection of *cinéma* in favor of *cinématographe*: "Films of the *cinéma* employ the resources of the theater (actors, direction, etc.) and use the camera to *reproduce*; those that employ the resources of the *cinématographe* use the camera to *create*."[2] Stressing the Greek root in the etymology of the word, Bresson views the *cinématographe* as a highly personal form of *écriture* and accentuates cinematic writing at the expense of *mise en scène*. He also proposes a precise film language of the "ineffable": "Your camera not only captures physical movements, it also captures certain states of the soul."[3] Bresson reiterates this idea, and emphasizes the uniqueness of his medium in an interview with Jacques Doniol-Valcroze and

---

[1] Paul Schrader, "Robert Bresson, Possibly," *Film Comment* 13 (September 1977), p. 26.

[2] Robert Bresson, *Notes sur le cinématographe* (Paris: Gallimard, 1975), p. 17.

[3] Ibid., p. 106.

Jean-Luc Godard: "The *cinématographe* is able to capture what words cannot say, what shapes and colors cannot render."[4] Bresson's goal, then, is to express the invisible through the most visually concrete of all media—to capture the inner lives of his characters as well as their spiritual destiny.

Most of Bresson's films are adaptations of pre-existing works, starting with *Les Dames du Bois de Boulogne* (1945), which is based on the Madame de la Pommeraye episode of Diderot's *Jacques le fataliste*. Next, Bresson adapted *Journal d'un curé de campagne* (1951) and *Mouchette* (1967) from novels by Bernanos—these two works and their cinematic counterparts are the focus of the chapters that follow. He then chose novellas by Dostoevsky as his source for two films, "A Gentle Woman" for *Une femme douce* (1969) and "White Nights" for *Quatre nuits d'un rêveur* (1971), followed by Tolstoy's "The Counterfeit Note" for *L'Argent* (1983). Bresson created both story and script for *Pickpocket* (1959) and *Au hasard Balthasar* (1966), though respectively they contain echoes from Dostoevsky's *Crime and Punishment* and *The Idiot*.

The filmmaker also found sources in historical material: *Un condamné à mort s'est échappé* (1956) is based on André Devigny's autobiographical account of his experience in a German prison camp, *Procès de Jeanne d'Arc* (1962) on the trial transcripts, and *Laneclot du Lac* (1974) on the Arthurian legends. Even though pre-existing texts were often the source of his films (due in part to temporal and financial constraints), Bresson stressed the importance of "putting himself" into them.[5]

The Jansenist doctrine of grace—the divine gift that reconciles the paradox of co-existing predestination and free will—has served as a filter for many critics in explaining Bresson's films: salvation and damnation depend on God's charity, the possibility of redemption depends on the mystery of God's grace. Bresson is preoccupied with spiritual grace, which is accorded to the protagonists of *Les Anges du péché* and *Journal d'un curé de campagne*, both religious subjects, but it is also found in the most unlikely of places: a pickpocket, an escaping prisoner, a donkey, a girl's suicide. André Bazin, conceivably the most important figure in the history of film criticism, describes the religious value of *Journal d'un curé de campagne* as a "phenomenology of salvation and grace," a formula which can be applied to all of Bresson's films through *Mouchette* (1967).[6] A pessimistic turn occurs, however, in Bresson's later works—particularly in his color films, which

---

[4] Robert Bresson, interview with Jacques Doniol-Valcroze and Jean-Luc Godard in *Cahiers du cinéma* 104 (February 1960), p. 6.

[5] Robert Bresson, interview with Jean-Luc Godard and Michel Delahaye in *Cahiers du cinéma* 178 (May 1966), p. 31.

[6] André Bazin, "Le *Journal d'un curé de campagne* et la stylistique de Robert Bresson," *Cahiers du cinéma* 3 (June 1951), p. 15.

include *Une femme douce* (1969), *Quatre nuits d'un rêveur* (1971), *Laneclot du Lac* (1974), *Le Diable probablement* (1977), and *L'Argent* (1983). Bresson's worldview becomes bleaker, salvation becomes damnation, the hope of redemption weakens, and the protagonists no longer experience saving grace.

Georges Bernanos, the second subject of these pages, provided the matter for two of Bresson's films. The first, *Journal d'un curé de campagne* (1936), was the *pièce de résistance* for both Bernanos and Bresson. The second Bernanos novel that Bresson filmed, *Nouvelle Histoire de Mouchette* (1937), was in its core a continuation of the world view expressed in the first novel/film. After that novel, Bernanos (temporarily) stopped writing fiction and moved into a darker political view of life expressed in his polemic essays —not unlike Bresson who likewise moved from a "light" to a "dark" view of life in his films after *Mouchette* (1967).

CHAPTER 1
The Hero's Spiritual Destiny in Bernanos'
Journal d'un curé de campagne

The Catholic faith is the fundamental element in the writing and life of author Georges Bernanos (1888–1948). His fiction, or self-labeled "Catholic realism," concerns the supernatural dimension of human existence, accessible only by communion with God. The key problematic in his novels does not necessarily concern the psychological or sociological traits of the characters, but rather the consequences of the absence or presence of God in their existence and of their struggle between two spiritual poles, God and Satan.

Bernanos' religious fiction exposes a continual reflection on the Passion of Christ. From a Catholic perspective, most of his protagonists are figures of Christ who live out the Passion in some form. This figure appears specifically in three forms: Christ the child, Christ the poor man, and Christ in his Passion. These three images of Christ correspond to the spiritual conditions that dominate the inner lives of Bernanos' characters: childhood, poverty, and agony. In Catholic theology, these three conditions are interrelated through *dépouillement*: poverty, the gradual emptying of the soul in life, agony, the final emptying of the soul in death, and the secret of eternal childhood lying in possessing nothing so that through God all things are finally possessed.

As a young man, Bernanos studied at the Aire-sur-la-Lys seminary as the first step toward his intended ordination. Even though he abandoned this early vocation, the author remained captivated by the pastoral mission. Not surprisingly, the central characters of his major novels—*Sous le Soleil de Satan* (1926), *L'Imposture* (1927), *La Joie* (1929), *Journal d'un curé de campagne* (1936), and *Monsieur Ouine* (1943)—are priests. Bernanos connected his *vocation d'écrivain* with sacerdotal vocation: his writing was a priestly calling through which he could contribute to the salvation of souls (his readers) to lead them to the Kingdom of God.[1]

In January of 1935, Bernanos wrote to his publisher, Robert Vallery-Radot, outlining the plan of *Journal d'un curé de campagne*. The novel would be the diary of a young priest, *ce jeune saint*, and the struggles of his ministry: "he will have served God in the same measure that he believes he has failed."[2] It would then illustrate the Christian message of salvation in the

---

[1] Georges Bernanos, *Correspondance inédite* (Paris: Plon, 1971), p. 589.

[2] Ibid., p. 46.

face of failure and death. The two key problems in the literary text concern whether the curé d'Ambricourt can save the souls of any of his parishioners and whether he himself can be at peace: Bernanos resolves them in the central conversion scene and in the death scene at the end of the novel.

The curé's commitment to God is integral to his personality and makes it impossible to separate his character from this Christian dimension. The curé's love for God provides his motivation for existing and conveying this love to his parish is the goal of his mission. When the curé tells the countess in the conversion scene that "hell is no longer loving," he articulates the importance of love and its role in directing humanity to God rather than toward Satan.[3] If hell is the state of not loving, then heaven must be the state of loving. At the end of his life the curé is able to put his trust entirely in God, making his death a simple expression of his love for God "because human agony is above all an act of love" (1256). Throughout the novel, Bernanos associates the curé with Christ, though the nameless hero often fails to recognize the correlation—he is unable to see the connection between his own suffering and grace. The diary form provides not only the structural framework of the novel; it also serves as a literary device for depicting the workings of divine grace in the curé's life.

The Diary and the Curé's Inner World

The curé narrates the entire three-part novel, with the exception of the last two pages in which the defrocked Dufréty recounts the hero's dying moments in a letter addressed to the latter's mentor, the curé de Torcy.[4] In this sole first-person narrative of Bernanos' works, the thirty-year old protagonist records spiritual reflections, personal confidences, everyday concerns, extensive accounts of encounters with others, and brief descriptions of priestly duties. Through the pages of his diary, the curé discloses his sense of inadequacy, his spiritual crisis, his deteriorating health, and his acceptance of self and of his own death.

Bernanos uses the diary form to present his main character by getting "inside" the curé; the reader then encounters his world from within. Although he interacts with characters who represent alternative viewpoints, the curé's perspective dominates the novel, and his voice supercedes all others as he records his spiritual and physical transformation. Rather than share his innermost feelings and religious experiences with the other characters,

---

[3] Georges Bernanos, *Œuvres romanesques* (Paris: Gallimard, 1961), p. 1157. All translations are my own, based on this Pléiade edition of the novel.

[4] The first two parts of the novel take place in rural Ambricourt and the third in the city of Lille. Ambricourt is based on the village of Fressin, where the author spent his childhood vacations. Real place names found in the novel, such as Desvres, Fruges, Hesdin, Norenfontes, Saint-Vaast, Torcy, and Verchocq, identify the region as the department of Pas-de-Calais.

"thoughts he keeps to himself," the curé reserves them for his diary (1032). The pages of his *cahiers d'écolier* become the privileged space in which he reveals the agony of his spiritual crisis and physical suffering. In fact, his bodily pain increases as his religious crisis deepens, and several entries simultaneously represent spiritual and physical anguish.

While diarists often date each entry to keep a chronological record, the curé refers to only two dates: he begins his diary on November 25th and his last doctor's appointment takes place on the 15th of the month.[5] Since he dies the following morning in Dufréty's apartment, the reader discovers that the curé writes his diary from November 25th to February 16th. In addition, the curé seldom refers to the exact time of day—he gives only vague temporal indications such as "an hour ago," "this morning," and "yesterday"—so that it is often difficult to determine how much time has elapsed between the moment he experiences an event and the moment he writes it down.[6] At first, the curé decides to keep the diary as an "experiment" for only one year, at which point he plans to burn it (1035). At the end of the first part of the novel, however, the diarist writes: "I had better continue the experiment to the very end" (1049).

Though on occasion he resolves to "destroy" his diary, the curé gradually realizes that his pages sustain him and he must continue to write them (1117). His *cahiers* become a "hidden treasure" and chief support during his continuous torment (1223). After the countess's death, he recognizes the importance of his beloved pages, and is unable to leave them behind during his anticipated short absence in Lille. While the curé worries about being too attached to his diary, he finds "solace in confiding these secrets" (1049).[7] The diarist writes in his pages what he keeps from his friends—the curé de Torcy, Dr. Delbende, and Olivier—such as the "secret" of his diagnosis. The café owner in Lille (Madame Duplouy) is the only character who witnesses his act of writing: she assumes the curé is "preparing a sermon," when in fact he writes about his fatal diagnosis (1229).[8]

The curé's diary serves various functions. Writing in his diary means being honest with himself, allowing the curé to truthfully record and evaluate

---

[5] Dufréty's final letter is dated as "February 19…" (1258).

[6] The curé refers to the precise time of day in just three passages (1113, 1166, and 1242). The last of these examples marks the only heading to a diary entry: *Minuit chez M. Dufréty* (1242).

[7] Bernanos expressed his attachment to and affection for his novel: "While writing [*Journal d'un curé de campagne*] I dreamed more than once to keep it for myself—I wished to stuff it away in a drawer so that it would not surface until after my death," in *Correspondance* II, p. 49. The curé in the novel then imitates his creator: "I will stuff these pages away in a drawer and re-read them later" (1049).

[8] During this scene Madame Duplouy tells him (ironically): "At your age, you have your whole life ahead of you" (1229).

"the very humble, insignificant secrets of a very ordinary life" (1036). The curé seeks to write about himself with "an inflexible severity," evident in the tone of humility and self-deprecation with which he describes his own person in both his meditative passages and those in which he records dialogue (1036). The simple and insecure diarist admits that he lacks experience in worldly matters, refers to his awkwardness in social situations, and affirms that his sense of inadequacy is confirmed by his sickly appearance, which causes continual gossip in the village of Ambricourt. Writing with "complete candor" is also a means for the curé to express his self-doubt in terms of his priestly capabilities (1036). He neatly summarizes his sense of failure as a priest in referring to his "supernatural clumsiness" (1177).

For the curé, another important function of the journal is "examining his conscience" (1036). Writing is a way of "turning his attention inward," a means to self-knowledge (1171). Consequently, the diary allows the curé to clarify his feelings and to stabilize his emotions. Since his mind has a tendency to wander, the curé admits that when he stops writing, he "loses his bearings" (1171). The therapeutic pages of his diary then represent "a great relief" in allowing him to "concentrate his thoughts" (1223).

Related to this, the diary serves a mirror-like function. At the end of the first part of the novel, the curé writes: "As I sit here scribbling...I get the feeling of an invisible presence...of a friend made in my image, though distinct from me."[9] Since the curé is aware of this *présence invisible*, to which he also refers as an "imaginary listener" and "another conscience," then writing in his diary reveals his *expérience du double* because it allows him to see "a forgotten, rediscovered face" (1036). The diary provides a way of discovering that hidden consciousness—one he glimpses below his familiar self—and serves as a mirror through which the curé sees himself. (His "forgotten face" will be revealed near the end of the diary as that of his own youth.)

The curé's diary is also a means of communicating with God—the diarist hopes for it to be a "conversation with God, an extension of prayer" (1048). The curé implicitly defines the ultimate goal of writing his diary as finding "this supernatural knowledge of oneself in God," and his pages contain a continuous commentary about his relationship with God (1129). But sometimes this relationship is troubled or subject to interference. During his spiritual crisis, when the curé finds "little comfort in prayer" and feels the absence of God, he turns to his diary, which represents his only refuge (1131). The diary even acts as a sort of companion for the curé in that it takes away his solitude: he slips his pages into his pocket "to read them again on

---

[9] "Tandis que je griffonne ces pages...j'ai le sentiment d'une présence invisible...d'un ami fait à mon image, bien que distinct de moi" (1049).

his monotonous trips from one end of the parish to the other" (1171). It is important to emphasize the phrase "read them again" in this passage because throughout the text the curé re-reads his pages to seek comfort, to see himself clearly, and to judge what he views as mistakes made in attempting to fulfill his priestly mission.

In Gérard Genette's terms, the reader encounters both the "intradiegetic" narrative of the events recorded by the curé and the "extradiegetic" narrative of his act of recording those events. The diarist constantly refers to the act of writing, as well as to his physical state or frame of mind while writing. Throughout the pages of his diary, the curé not only records his spiritual reflections, but also comments on what he has written or what he is about to write: the act of writing the diary becomes part of his spiritual adventure, as he reflects on his own pages and on the problems of writing in general. (For example, he occasionally refers to the potential narcissism that accompanies the writing of a journal.) Although the curé claims that he will write exactly what comes into his mind, he still "searches for words" and corrects himself: writing in his diary clearly reveals an act of reflection (1049). If his lines about the conversion scene will "make an impression," it is because (as with most of his entries) the curé has reflected on and organized his thoughts about the episode before writing about it (1157).

In the second part of the novel, the curé recognizes that as the writer of his beloved pages, he is in effect an author. Dufréty, the curé's former classmate at the seminary, emerges as the other writer figure in the novel. The reader initially encounters him as a writer of letters, and the opposition good/bad writer surfaces when the curé offers a negative (literary) critique of Dufréty's first letter, disapproving of the "forced gaiety" in its tone (1058). The diarist then labels the style of Dufréty's second letter as "pathetic," and characterizes the writing in the third letter as "puerile, conceited, and void of any supernatural quality" (1063 and 1088).

Next, the reader encounters Dufréty as an aspiring autobiographical author. He tells the curé about his work in progress: "It's a kind of diary entitled *My Stages*. My case should be of interest to many people" (1247). The very title of the self-obsessed writer's work (in contrast to the curé's selflessness) evokes the opposite notion of the curé's first words in his diary, "my parish" (1031). In addition, Dufréty's claim to write with honesty pales in comparison with the "sincerity" of the curé's writing (1117). Dufréty's arrogance, air of intellectual superiority, and need for self-justification, evident in his letters (and conversation), and which he would presumably record in his autobiographical work, contrast with the humble quality of the curé's diary. Furthermore, in his letter to Torcy describing the last moments of the curé's life, Dufréty reveals his plan to use the curé's diary to enhance his own literary career (1258). The curé's humility is in contrast with

Dufréty's vanity, just as his "saintliness" opposes Dufréty's mediocrity—the diarist describes him as a "mediocre priest" (1090). As a failed priest and self-seeking writer, both a *prêtre manqué* and an *écrivain manqué*, Dufréty embodies the negative image of the hero's dual vocation as *curé-écrivain*.[10]

Throughout his diary the curé not only comments on his own writing, he also problematizes language. He argues that Catholics use a "vocabulary filled with terms worn so smooth by constant use" that it allows them to justify everything and question nothing (1061). When they go to confession, then, this vocabulary encourages them to avoid a true examination of conscience: the curé compares this kind of language to "a dirty window pane, so blurred that nothing can be seen clearly" (1099). Near the end of the novel, he refers to a "language that is no longer Christian" because it consists only of a few well-worn sayings and phrases from newspapers (1229).

The curé also critiques language by presenting another metaphor in which he compares words to a "lock" used only for its basic function (1061–62). In trying to express the spiritual in his pages, he attempts to rejuvenate language to achieve that expression. For example, he regrets that he cannot adequately articulate his spiritual despair. After writing the word *tristesse* to convey this despair, the curé adds: "Unfortunately I can find no other word to describe this indefinable weakness, as though my own soul were bleeding. I awoke with a start, with a loud cry ringing in my ears. But was it really a cry? Is that the word for it?"[11]

The diarist frequently stresses the insufficiency of words throughout his meditative passages. He often hesitates in writing a word or regrets having written a word in his persistent search for the *mot juste*: "I wish I hadn't written the word 'pride' and yet I cannot cross it out—there is no other to express a state of mind so human."[12] The curé also writes: "The expression 'to lose one's faith,' as one loses a purse or a key ring, has always seemed foolish to me.... Keep silent, what a strange expression! Silence keeps us."[13]

---

[10] Dr. Laville (the physician who gives the curé his fatal diagnosis in the last part) is another "negative double" of the curé. He notes their physical resemblance, and compares his drug addiction to the curé's act of praying. The latter rejects this comparison by declaring that he does not look for "forgetfulness in prayer, but strength" (1236). Dr. Delbende (a friend of Torcy) and Olivier (the countess's nephew), on the other hand, are "positive doubles" of the curé.

[11] "Je ne trouve malheureusement pas d'autre mot pour qualifier une défaillance qui ne peut se définir, une véritable hémorragie de l'âme. Je m'éveillais brusquement avec, dans l'oreille, un grand cri—mais est-ce encore ce mot-là qui convient?" (1099).

[12] "Je regrette un peu d'avoir écrit le mot d'orgueil, et cependant je ne puis l'effacer, faute d'en trouver un qui convienne mieux à un sentiment si humain" (1054). In a later passage, the curé regrets the fact that the "word would not be right (*le mot ne serait pas juste*)" (1222).

[13] "Cette expression de 'perdre sa foi' comme on perd sa bourse ou un trousseau de clefs m'a toujours paru un peu niaise.... Garder le silence, quel mot étrange! C'est le silence qui nous garde" (1125 and 1229).

The diarist even uses scientific language to express his spiritual reflections. In describing the identity of his parish, the curé employs terminology from the field of physics: he compares good and evil to "two liquids of different density" (1031). In another example, the curé uses geological imagery in describing sin as a "thin film over an ocean of liquid fire" (1090).

After the curé shows his mentor a few pages of his diary, but does not reveal its authorship, the curé de Torcy describes them as "too well written" (1066). He then offers the young curé a caution about writing (down one's thoughts), which should be done objectively: "You see a thing just as it is, without setting music to it, so there is no risk of singing a song for yourself alone."[14] To some extent, Torcy is right. For the curé, the most dangerous aspect of writing is recording the darkest moments of his spiritual crisis.

On six occasions in the text, the curé must struggle to confide his anguished thoughts: several pages are missing because he has torn them out. The reader is informed of these deletions by a fictional editor, who serves as a literary device used by Bernanos to convince the reader of the diary's reality. The omitted pages function as a sign of the curé's inner, spiritual turmoil, and before a deletion his writing usually reflects a mood of agony or dark thoughts. For example, before the first omission he admits to thinking of himself "as of a dead person" (1114). The fictional editor then steps in to inform the reader that ten pages have been ripped out of the *cahier*.[15] Next, we read a short paragraph (highlighted by blank spaces and single-dotted lines) in which the curé records Dr. Delbende's death, thought to be a suicide. At this point, the diarist explains his desire to "destroy" the journal, but upon "thinking it over," he only disposes of those pages which seem to be "useless"; in any case, he admits to knowing them by heart (1114).

The next time the fictional editor steps in, he informs the reader that certain lines have been crossed out but are still legible. In these lines the curé asserts that he will not love himself again because he can only "love himself through God," whom he has momentarily lost: "God is silent—silence" (1129). The curé then admits writing these lines about God's absence in a "moment of overwhelming agony" (1129). At the height of this feeling of spiritual emptiness, reflected in the silence of God, the curé crosses out lines that are witness to his agony. After his most significant deletion—the curé presumably omits his confession about the temptation to commit suicide —he again offers an explanation for the torn-out pages: "Though I have now

---

[14] "On voit la chose telle quelle, sans musique, et on ne risque pas de se chanter une chanson pour soi tout seul" (1067).

[15] The fictional editor appears several times to inform the reader that lines have been crossed out, phrases have been added in the margins, and pages have been ripped out. In Sartre's *La Nausée* (published two years after *Journal*), a fictional editor also comments on missing pages: the diarist's mental torment causes him to destroy parts of his text.

decided never to destroy this diary, I felt bound to take out these pages, written in a veritable delirium."[16]

The suppressed passages reflect the curé's agony and despair brought on by the absence of God, and mark his attempt to censor personal doubts about his vocation. He is not only carrying the heavy burdens of his parish (taking upon himself the sin and suffering of others), but also those of his illness. The reader assumes that the torn-out pages contain the curé's experience of an insufferable amount of human pain. The pages are then "useless" because they focus on his own pain and suffering (1114). The curé realizes this is contradictory to his vocation, which demands that he suffer for others. At the end of his diary, he recognizes that his vocation demands a complete gift of self. Thus he tears out pages to avoid self-pity in keeping with his priestly (and perhaps saint-like) quality of selflessness. The fact that the curé's name in the novel is simply that of his parish signifies his self-effacement.

It is possible, however, to look at the deletion question in another way. Why would the curé omit anything if "no one will ever read" his pages (1049)? The question of readership arises when he suggests that there may be other readers/commentators of the diary aside from the diarist himself. Clearly he anticipates the existence of an eventual reader or unnamed recipient of his pages: "If these pages were to be seen by indifferent eyes, [the reader] would surely find me to be naive.... In reading these lines, [the reader] would think that my words were part of a general plan—I swear they were not."[17] In another example, the curé expresses self-deprecation about his priestly abilities by claiming to be a "danger to souls": "And who, after reading these miserable pages, every line of which reveals my weakness... who would not understand?"[18] Although the curé claims that in his diary he writes only private thoughts, he frequently shows concern for the fate of his journal and for any potential reader's response to it. He insists that his diary may become useful not only for himself, but for a "future reader" as well (1117). Bernanos keeps the curé's innermost spiritual state a secret from the other characters, but not from us, *futurs lecteurs* and implied readers.

The diary form not only provides the reader access to the curé's inner feelings, it also enables Bernanos to contrast the curé's perceptions with those of the reader. While the curé writes about the failure of his pastoral mission, the reader knows that the curé succeeds in saving the soul of and

---

[16] "Résolu que je suis à ne pas détruire ce journal, [j'ai] cru devoir faire disparaître ces pages écrites dans un véritable délire" (1184).

[17] "Si ces lignes pouvaient tomber un jour sous des regards indifférents, on me trouverait assurément bien naïf.... A lire ces lignes, on pensera sans doute que je suivais un plan. Il n'en était rien, je le jure" (1064 and 1159).

[18] "Qui ne comprendrait d'ailleurs, ne serait-ce qu'à la lecture de ces pages misérables où ma faiblesse...éclate à chaque ligne!" (1141).

communicating his faith to at least one parishioner, the countess. Although Bernanos stays "within" the hero, he is able to suggest ideas that go beyond the humble curé's thoughts—the "future reader" so often evoked or implied can find Catholic or liturgical symbolism (about which the curé does not comment) in certain events recorded by the diarist.

The Diary and the Outside World

The first words of the novel reveal the external focus of the curé's diary, his parish. In the opening paragraphs, the diarist reflects on his parish by evoking the metaphorical "cancer" of evil and sin—*l'ennui*—that devours it (1031). The curé writes other metaphors concerning *l'ennui*, the inner condition of a world without faith, to convey its "inescapable presence" in his parish (1032 and 1143). As this parish represents a typical one of the French rural world, it has fallen victim to what the curé (and Bernanos) view as the decline of moral and spiritual values: it is stuck "in the mud" of moral and religious weariness, and its parishioners are part of a "Christianity in decay" (1032). Throughout his diary the curé will present his parish as being in need of redemption.[19]

The curé repeats the phrase "my parish (*ma paroisse*)" in the beginning of the novel so that the reader immediately identifies the writer of the diary as the guardian of his parish. As the curé contemplates the village from atop a hill, he compares his suffering parish to a flock, and records the image of a "shepherd" who can guide his flock and lead it to safety (1031–32). This passage suggests that the curé must take on the role of shepherd/Christ-figure to lead his flock/parishioners away from the cancer of sin and evil.

On numerous pages of his diary the curé records his own suffering from a sickness related to his stomach, which forces him to digest only bread and wine as nourishment. This illness is finally diagnosed as stomach cancer, which causes the curé's death. On the first page of his journal the curé describes his parish as being consumed by the same disease with which he himself is diagnosed; the curé is ravaged by cancer and thus literally assumes the cancer of his parish. He continuously takes on the suffering of his parishioners by imitating Christ, "who suffers our pain, takes joy in our happiness, will share our last hour and receive us into His arms, upon His heart" (1051). To imitate Christ is to "suffer for souls," to suffer on behalf of others.[20] For example, during his crucial encounter, *rencontre*, with the

---

[19] The city dwellers of Lille are also in need of redemption: in his description of the anonymous masses of the crowded urban streets (recalling Baudelaire), the curé clings to his religious perspective in viewing the city as a center of spiritual misery.

[20] The diarist often repeats the phrase *souffrir par les âmes* (1052, 1054, and 1226). In an important dialogue between the curé and Dr. Delbende, Bernanos indicates that the hero's struggle with his ancestors' alcoholism, like his stomach cancer, suggests vicarious suffering

countess's daughter, Chantal, the curé is willing to accept in himself the suffering she endures: "I could hardly bear such sadness and yet I was anxious to share it, to assume it in its entirety, to let it flood my heart, my soul, my bones, my whole being."[21] By accepting her burden and presenting himself in sacrifice, the curé's sense of God's presence briefly returns as he once again experiences "the blessed quiet wherein the voice of God can be heard—God speaks" (1135). The curé also "communes with" Dr. Delbende's suffering, and essentially assumes the latter's anguish (1096). A transference of agony occurs in the narration: the doctor's suffering is replaced with that of the curé.

The second meditative passage containing the curé's reflections on his parish chronicles the deep love he feels for it, to which he strives to give himself entirely, as the very phrase *ma paroisse* fills his heart "with tenderness" (1052). Here the key to his reflection on "the eyes" of his parish concerns the hidden gaze of humanity, as it was first seen by Christ "from the Cross" (1052). Through this vision of the world below him, Christ prayed for its forgiveness. It is important to stress the presence of two gazes in this passage: the *regard* of the parish (which becomes the *regard* of humanity) and that of the curé, who unknowingly identifies himself with Christ. According to the diarist, his parish looks at him pleadingly for a guide, and his gaze is one of love and forgiveness: "Forgive them for they know not what they do" (1052 and Luke 23:24).

The curé deepens his reflections about his parish in a third meditative passage, where he again observes the village from a hilltop (1061–62). This viewpoint, from which he imagines he can reach out and embrace his parish, marks the very place where he first contemplated writing his diary. There, looking down on his parish, after making his rounds through it, the curé conceived of keeping a simple account of his daily journeys and experiences within that world. As in the earlier entry, the curé hopes to see the *regard* of his parish, but it fails to respond: "I look down, but it never seems to look back at me.... What does it want from me?"[22] While the curé feels alienated from his parish, he yearns to "possess" it, suggesting his hope to save his parishioners. The curé imagines that they have "nailed him to a cross" (signifying an additional identification with Christ)—his parishioners require

---

(1091–92). Other characters, however, believe the curé drinks "alone, in hiding" (1205) because they often catch him in the act of drinking wine at the rectory (1124, 1174, 1175, and 1190).

[21] "Je pouvais à peine soutenir cette tristesse, et en même temps, je souhaitais de la partager, de l'assumer toute entière, qu'elle me pénétrât, remplît mon cœur, mon âme, mes os, mon être" (1135).

[22] "Je le regarde, et je n'ai jamais l'impression qu'il me regarde aussi.... Que me veut-il?" (1060–61).

Christ-like suffering, and the curé longs to see their faces as Christ saw humanity in the midst of his agony on the cross.

Throughout his diary the young curé strives to determine his role as priest in relation to his parish and looks to the elder curé de Torcy for help.[23] He longs for Torcy's "health, courage, and balance," hoping to emulate his mentor whom he describes as a man of prayer, a strong leader of his parish, and a "true servant of God" (1036 and 1191). The curé de Torcy argues for a practical approach to the priestly mission: a priest can only hope to achieve the limited goal of "commanding his parish, maintaining order, and perhaps inspiring respect" (1038). The lesson taught by Torcy is to trust God's will (with a child-like faith) and to imitate Christ's own simplicity (1091–92). He acknowledges that a priest's task is a difficult one in that he must fulfill the spiritual needs of his parishioners with little reward in return.

The curé also learns from Torcy that the true mission of the church is to bring joy, and in the young priest's mind his personal mission is to show the truth of God's love. But how can he fulfill this mission when his parish rejects him and fails to form a religious community? The words of Arsène the sacristan represent the spiritual indifference of the parish: "A priest is like a notary—he's there if you need him.... [but] when you're dead, you're dead."[24] The younger generation, represented by the hostile children in catechism class for whom the curé's heart fills "with tenderness," resists his efforts to raise the spiritual life of his parish (1050). The curé's agony comes in part from what he views as a futile struggle to uplift his parish. For all the energy he pours into his work, little seems accomplished.

While the curé finds himself in an unloving parish, he never stops trying to reach out to his parishioners, and even hours before dying he still thinks about caring for them. The curé is determined to make rounds with a frequency well beyond the call of duty and struggles to assume his priestly obligations, although his rapidly declining health makes his daily work increasingly difficult. His recurring and persistent stomach pains multiply the hours spent on the road since he is unable to use his bicycle on inclines. Yet if he cannot get out among his flock as he would like to do, the parishioners, for the most part, do not come to him—at daily mass the church would be empty if not for the presence of Chantal's governess, Mlle. Louise.

---

[23] For the most part, the curé takes on the passive role of listener in dialogues with Torcy (1036–47, 1066–80, 1101–03, 1117–23, 1185–89, and 1190–94): the elder priest rarely allows his friend to express an opinion. With the countess, her daughter Chantal, and young Séraphita, however, the curé exercises his sacerdotal functions by speaking, for the most part, with "confidence and abundance" (1142).

[24] "Un curé est comme un notaire. Il est là en cas de besoin.... quand on est mort tout est mort" (1182).

The curé records his visits with parishioners in greater detail than any of his other priestly duties. While he briefly alludes to routine aspects of his ministry, such as daily mass, confession, funerals, and catechism class, the curé does not perform the sacraments of baptism, marriage, and last rites in the novel. (Other sacraments such as holy communion and confirmation are implied in his references to daily mass and catechism class.) Furthermore, the curé never mentions the season of Advent (during which he begins the journal), Christmas, the Feast of the Holy Family, nor the Feast of the Epiphany (which take place in December and January). He does allude to All Saints Day, but the liturgical calendar is practically absent from the novel: the curé's encounters or spiritual confrontations with certain parishioners reveal his true sacerdotal function. Of these, the scene of the countess's conversion represents a major turning point in the curé's life; it marks the beginning of his own spiritual regeneration. Before this scene, he chronicles his inability to become a "true leader of his parish, a guardian of souls," yet the encounter between the curé and the countess reveals that he acts as God's instrument in bringing her salvation (1141).

In the first half of the novel, the curé struggles with his parishioners' failure to accept God. His attempts to express his religious convictions in the pulpit and in catechism class fail, as the parishioners respond only with contempt and mockery. At first he feels merely inadequate, but he approaches despair when confronted with the realization that his parish rejects him—an anonymous letter demanding his immediate departure, "the sooner the better," marks the climax of this rejection (1110). The curé's sense of failure as a priest is accompanied by inner spiritual crisis: he feels isolated not only from his parish, but separated from God as well. As a result, he loses the ability to pray, which is needed "as much as air to draw breath" or oxygen to fill his blood (1111). But the curé's spiritual emptiness becomes fullness during his *rencontre* with the countess. If he has (temporarily) lost the *effrayante présence* of God, he finds it again during the countess episode by recapturing "the spirit of prayer" (1034 and 1161).

The curé's decisive encounter with Chantal, the countess's adolescent daughter, functions as a prelude to the conversion scene (1131–39).[25] Chantal comes to the curé of her own will to reveal the conflict beneath the surface of her upper-class family's exterior: her governess Mlle. Louise is her father's mistress. In divulging her deep hatred for the woman who has replaced her in her father's affections, it appears at first that Chantal is asking the curé to intercede on her behalf. Yet when the curé asks why she lives in a state of revolt against love, Chantal replies ferociously that she "hates everyone" (1136). (In his second encounter with Chantal, which takes place after the

---

[25] This encounter takes place in the sacristy, the confessional, and the cemetery.

countess's death, the curé tells her that she hates only herself, marking her refusal to give herself to God.)

Throughout the novel the curé "reads" the souls of his parishioners, perceiving their inner state, and in this scene he detects "the power of evil and sin" on Chantal's face (1138). The curé continually records the hardness or *dureté* of her face, which corresponds to her spiritual emptiness and her rejection of the curé's efforts to help her. He will describe those who suffer in hell, who have lost the capacity to love, in terms of hardness during the conversion scene. In identifying the lovelessness in the heart of Chantal's mother, the curé will have a vision of the countess's death that her hardness would make eternal.

The curé's vision of Chantal's hardness marks the first example of his clairvoyance in this scene. In the second example, the curé "reads" words on her lips, other than those she pronounces. His spiritual insight enables him to "read" Chantal's soul and perceive her hidden intentions: she is in fact threatening to take her life. In the third example, the curé perceives a letter that he cannot see, which presumably contains Chantal's plan for revenge against her father. (The curé will burn this unread letter.) After asking her for the letter, Chantal exclaims that the curé "must be the devil" (1137). His power to "see" into her soul is, on the contrary, a way of imitating Christ. The curé does not view these events as divine or supernatural works. For the (Catholic) reader, however, these examples of profound intuition or supernatural insight reveal the presence of God, and extend well beyond what the curé labels as the "insignificant secrets" of his "ordinary" life (1036).

At the climax of their confrontation, the curé tells Chantal that she is an accomplice of sin as a member of the "communion of sinners": sinners unite in "their hatred and contempt" to become a "lake of mud over which the vast tide of divine love passes in vain" (1139). Here Bernanos depicts the reality of evil through the image of mud, which echoes the curé's earlier words to Chantal—he told her that she herself is "no more than mud" (1138). After this encounter, the curé awakens with the "impression, even the certainty," of having heard someone call his name: in vain, he looks around the garden (1140). This *appel manqué* suggests his failure to perform his ultimate sacerdotal function, his inability to save Chantal's soul. Although the curé fails to draw out the evil in Chantal, he will succeed with her mother.

The Conversion Scene

The curé's "distressing encounter" with Chantal becomes an "extraordinary encounter" with her mother (1130 and 1161).[26] The countess episode or

---

[26]Daughter and mother exhibit similar behavior during their confrontations with the curé, who uses the same terms to describe their trembling, laughter, and stamping of the feet (1133–62).

conversion scene, which takes place during the curé's third visit to the chateau, marks the longest scene in the novel as well as its climax (1145–64). The significance of the conversion scene is apparent in the number of pages Bernanos devotes to it and in its placement at the center of the novel. In addition, the pages that come before the countess episode can be seen as preparatory to it, and those that follow chronicle the repercussions of the climactic scene.

The scene moves step by step toward the countess's conversion. Initially she shows a kind of skeptical resistance, but once engaged in the dialogue, as the curé becomes more eloquent and self-assured, her resistance to him dissolves. First, she recounts the entire story of her family's hatred. Once her "confession" is complete, the countess no longer appears a participant in a vicious family conflict; rather she is wrestling with God, and at the same time struggling for salvation. The next step takes place when the curé realizes the nature of her struggle, and in the final step the countess wins the struggle for salvation. Though at first the curé accuses her of not loving her daughter, their *rencontre* unveils the presence of a more profound spiritual problem, the noblewoman's hatred of God.

Early in the dialogue, the countess reveals her husband's infidelity and her own refusal to help ease her daughter's suffering.[27] But there is more. The curé senses the countess's state of anguish as she struggles to let him know "her unfortunate secret" (1148)—the death of her infant son, for whom she has grieved for eleven years. This death has left the countess in a state of hopelessness: she bitterly resents anyone who might intrude upon the emotional isolation into which she has withdrawn. Her secret has caused her own spiritual death, evident in her despair and her hatred of God.

When the curé understands that the countess's hatred reveals her spiritual void, the terms of their *rencontre* shift: she is no longer just a distraught and resentful mother, but a parishioner who rebels against God. The countess feels that "God has taken everything" from her through the death of her son (1156). This cause of her anguish then provokes an important discussion of hell, which contrasts with the scene's central motif of God's love: according to the curé, the countess's refusal to love will separate her from her son for all eternity because "hell is no longer loving (*l'enfer c'est de ne plus aimer*)" (1157). The conflict between hate and love reveals the battle between Satan and God: the curé's inner voice describes the former as the enemy who con-

---

[27] Even when the curé informs her of Chantal's desire to commit suicide—a desire he will "read" in the soul of the countess herself (1160)—the mother refuses to see how she can help her daughter. Upon hearing himself tell the countess that God forbids her to push her daughter to despair, the curé realizes that he must press on "to the very end" in order to eliminate the spiritual cancer within the countess (1146).

fronts his adversary of grace or divine presence. The curé's goal, then, is to shift the weight from the forces of malevolence to the forces of benevolence.

Through the literary device of dialogue Bernanos presents a discussion on the nature and function of love: the curé tells the countess (and the reader) that the faculty of loving is not only inseparable from our being, it is also the pathway to salvation and God. The countess asks how she can be separated from her son for all eternity if she loves him, and the curé replies that in order to love, she must not reject God's love. While the countess attempts in vain to argue that nothing can separate her "from the one she loved more than life," she will ultimately succumb to the curé's reasoning: "God is love itself—if you want to love, don't place yourself beyond love's reach."[28]

As the countess's rebellion erupts in response to the curé's command that she resign herself to God and "open her heart to Him," the curé notes her final words as an unbeliever: she declares that God has become "indifferent" to her (1159–60). Before the moment of conversion occurs, the diarist records his sudden fear that he has been tricked by Chantal, and has recklessly confronted her mother. But he quickly dismisses these alternatives and comes to recognize the supernatural quality of the episode: "There are no words to describe it...the spirit of prayer came back into my heart."[29] The curé's rare observations about what takes place in the outside world, particularly on the grounds and in the kitchen of the chateau—sounds and images that occur in "everyday life" (1164)—contrast with the spiritual quality of the episode. The great struggle for the countess's soul takes place "at the extreme limit of the invisible world" (1169).

The conversion starts with the countess's physical surrender: she sinks into a chair and withdraws from her bosom a medallion containing a lock of her son's hair. Her submission begins when she grasps the importance of the curé's words: "You cannot bargain with God—we must give ourselves to Him unconditionally."[30] Again the curé's inner voice returns to explain his re-found sureness of God's presence after his own period of spiritual conflict: "A mysterious hand struck a breach in an invisible rampart so that peace flowed in from every side...a peace unknown to the earth."[31] Now that the countess believes, she renounces her previous thoughts, and relinquishes her hold on hatred by performing the cathartic act of recounting the death of her infant son. (She even asks the curé to repeat his key expression about hell as the state of "no longer loving.") At this point the curé finally acknowledges

---

[28] "Dieu est l'amour même—si vous voulez aimer, ne vous mettez pas hors de l'amour" (1158).

[29] "Cela ne peut s'exprimer...l'esprit de prière rentra en moi" (1161).

[30] "On ne marchande pas avec le bon Dieu, il faut se rendre à lui, sans condition" (1161).

[31] "Une main mystérieuse venait d'ouvrir une brèche dans on ne sait quelle muraille invisible, et la paix rentrait de toutes parts...une paix inconnue de la terre" (1162).

his role as the intermediary through whom the countess confesses to God. He
furthers her reconciliation with God by having her repeat lines of the Our
Father: at last she prays "Thy kingdom come" (1163). This reconciliation
brings about the resolution of the loss of her son, as the curé informs the
countess that the kingdom for which she prays belongs to her and her son.

By throwing the medallion into the fire in a gesture of resignation, the
countess believes she can redeem her hatred through this sacrificial act, as
she seems to take the curé's words literally: "Give your pride with all the rest
—give everything!"[32] The curé retrieves the medallion from the fire, burning
his arm, and exclaims that God is not an "executioner"; rather God wants us
to be merciful with ourselves and takes "our pain upon Himself" (1164). In
the beginning of the episode the curé had told the countess: "I am every-
body's servant...or should I say a thing to be used by everyone...if God so
wills it."[33] He then becomes *une chose* when he thrusts his arm into the fire to
retrieve the medallion, given this comment about the poker: "It is only an
instrument in your hands. Had God endowed it with just enough consciousness to place itself into your hands whenever you needed it, that would be
more or less what I am for you."[34] Thus the curé offers himself to the countess as an instrument put into her hands, like the poker, by God.[35] After
retrieving the medallion, he endorses her reconciliation with God: "You are
at peace, my daughter."[36] In reflecting on this pastoral blessing, the curé
evokes their shared (divine) peace in that it also has descended upon him.

After the conversion scene, the curé receives a letter (along with the
medallion) in which the countess expresses her gratitude to him in the most
sincere terms. She explains that he gave her hope by "resurrecting" her dead
child, and concludes by assuring him that he also gave her peace (1165–66).
In the entry following the transcription of the countess's treasured letter, the
curé records her death (presumably of heart failure) in a single line,
highlighted by blank spaces: his benediction has become an absolution.

The conversion provides spiritual release not only for the countess, but
for the curé as well; he feels joyous upon leaving the chateau. Writing from a
retrospective vantage point after the countess's death, the curé realizes his
role in reconciling a soul to hope, which he receives in return: "Hope, which
was shrinking in my heart, flowered again in hers—the spirit of prayer,

---

[32] "Donnez votre orgueil avec le reste, donnez tout!" (1163).

[33] "Moi, je suis le serviteur de tous...je devrais dire la chose de tous...s'il plait à Dieu" (1146).

[34] "Ce tisonnier n'est qu'un instrument dans vos mains. Si le bon Dieu lui avait donné juste assez
de connaissance pour se mettre de lui-même à votre portée, lorsque vous en avez besoin, ce serait
à peu près ce que je suis pour vous" (1146).

[35] Another everyday object acquires a spiritual significance in this scene: the countess breaks a
fan that she nervously holds in her hand, symbolizing the anguish of her inner struggle (1150).

[36] "Soyez donc en paix, ma fille" (1164).

which I thought lost in me, was given back to her by God and, who can tell, perhaps in my name."[37] The episode allows him to (again) experience God's presence, guidance, and redemptive work, as the curé directly addresses God: "I am stripped bare of all things, Lord, as you alone can strip us bare, for nothing escapes your extraordinary care, nor your extraordinary love."[38]

It is significant that only the curé and the countess know the true nature of what transpires during the conversion scene. Their dialogue occurs with the traditional confidentiality of the confessional—even though it takes place in the salon of the chateau—so that they symbolically take on roles of confessor and confessee.[39] Still, the *rencontre* between the curé and the countess becomes public knowledge because of Chantal's eavesdropping: her version of the story spreads to the count, the village, the church hierarchy, and finally to the curé de Torcy. The count's uncle, the Canon de la Motte-Beuvron, asks the curé to "write a few lines" about the encounter, seeking in part to protect the family name after the countess's "sudden" death (1173).[40] This request is simply a political gesture to pacify the hierarchy since no one will read those lines (unlike those of the diary). Given that the curé has sworn silence to the countess, he refuses to write a statement, rendering the canon's mediation unsuccessful.

Since Chantal has misunderstood the conversation, claiming that the episode left her mother in turmoil, the curé has to endure the parishioners' harsh criticism of the encounter and even that of the curé de Torcy. The young curé refuses to show his friend the countess's letter, as he discloses its contents only in his diary.[41] (After this scene, Torcy appears in the novel only one more time. Bernanos removes the curé's perspective from the dialogue with his mentor in which it was initially involved: Torcy has guided him to the point where he must continue his personal mission on his own.) While Bernanos seems to suggest alternative interpretations of the countess episode, through the disapproval of the count, the Canon, and Torcy, they fail to challenge the curé's authentic account of the event in his diary. The reader

---

[37] "L'espérance qui se mourait dans mon cœur a refleuri dans le sien, l'esprit de prière que j'avais cru perdu sans retour, Dieu le lui a rendu, et qui sait? En mon nom peut-être" (1170).

[38] "Me voilà dépouillé, Seigneur, comme vous seul savez dépouiller, car rien n'échappe à votre sollicitude effrayante, à votre effrayant amour" (1170).

[39] The curé reminds the countess: "I am your priest, your pastor.... I speak to you as a priest, according to the light that God has given me" (1155–58). The latter line foretells the meditative passage in which he expresses his hope to "bring light into the innermost recess" of her consciousness (1160).

[40] Before meeting with the Canon, the curé learns that the countess had "suffered from heart disease" (1167).

[41] At one point, however, the count picks up the letter from under the curé's table. He then hands it to the curé, who assumes that the countess's husband has not noticed the handwriting (1176).

has privileged access to this account, and has read the full transcription of the countess's letter: s/he knows that the curé has experienced a peace that comes only from God in acknowledging his role as divine intermediary.

The countess episode provides a specific example of salvation in Bernanosian fiction. The curé acts as God's instrument in bringing it to the countess, releasing her from her hatred of God and helping her to win "this great fight for eternal life" (1169). Although earlier in his diary the curé records his self-doubt and sense of failure concerning his encounters with parishioners, he feels confident that he has served God during the conversion episode: "Our Lord needed a witness, and I was chosen."[42] Nonetheless, he feels undeserving: "It is too much that God should have given me the grace to be present when a soul became reconciled to hope."[43]

And yet, the curé experiences great agony after the conversion scene, resulting from his willingness to suffer on behalf of his parishioners, to take the burden of their sins upon himself. The curé told the countess that even if the "most contemptible of the living" were cast into the burning depths of hell, he would take the latter from his "executioner" in order to "share his suffering" (1157). During their confrontation, the countess's head seemed "to bend as under an invisible weight"; images of heaviness then shift to the curé (1159). In blessing the lifeless countess, his hands feel like "lead," and upon reading her letter again, he feels as if the countess's "burden" has been placed upon his shoulders by God (1184). Thus he becomes a Christ-figure in his redemption of the countess's burden and acceptance of her suffering.

The last two in the sequence of nights of the curé's experience of agony occur after the countess's death. These nights fill the curé's heart with anguish as he begins to realize that agony—the agony that Christ bore—is an "essential condition" of the human soul (1183). The end of the countess's agony marks the return of his own, as the curé takes on the countess's sin and suffering. This sacrifice, he realizes, has its "price" (1184): "We pay a heavy, very heavy price for the superhuman dignity of our calling."[44] The price is the acceptance of the agony from which the other is delivered: the burden of suffering that has been lifted from the shoulders of the countess descends on the curé with all its weight.

Light, Childhood, Poverty: God's Grace

Darkness and agony are gradually replaced by the light of the curé's last mornings in Ambricourt, which are "blessed by God's grace" (1208). As a

---

[42] "Notre-Seigneur avait besoin d'un témoin, et j'ai été choisi" (1168).

[43] "C'est déjà trop que Dieu m'ait fait la grâce d'assister à cette réconciliation d'une âme avec l'espérance" (1168).

[44] "Nous payons cher, très cher, la dignité surhumaine de notre vocation" (1089).

result, the curé feels better and is able to pray better: "Like the village, my prayer has no more weight to it."[45] The light motif gains more significance in the crucial (morning) scene with Olivier, the countess's nephew, as the curé's motorcycle ride with his new friend introduces him to a world of pure light: "The roar of the engine rose continuously higher until it gave out only one note, extraordinarily pure. It was like the song of light, it was light itself."[46] It is important to stress that this passage marks the progression from the material (the sound of the engine) to the spiritual (the mystical dimension of pure light), and that the curé associates this experience full of light with childhood.

The Olivier episode and its subsequent effects upon the curé reveal the importance of *l'esprit d'enfance* in Bernanosian fiction. According to the author's vision, childhood represents the quality of unspoiled purity into which one is born; it is the state of soul identified with grace.[47] The youth recognized by the curé during the Olivier episode is the one he never experienced. The curé realizes that he has never been young; his life was so weighed down with misery and poverty that there was no time for childhood. In his vision of a world bathed in light, the curé grasps the meaning of that childhood which has passed him by. He feels an unexpected reassurance that God does not want him to die before "tasting the risk of youth" just once (1211). In the curé's eyes, Olivier's machine is a "magical toy" that poor boys see only in their dreams (1212). This dream comes true, as the curé feels truly young for the first time: he acknowledges that his present happiness is a God-given moment of the childhood he never had, a reflection of the "joy" that belongs to that same childhood as it is "regained through grace" (1212).

The Olivier episode marks not only the curé's journey into a domain of light; it also foreshadows his access to paradise since the motorcycle ride opens "the door to another world" (1213). It is important to stress that this episode begins on a hilltop, recalling the earlier hilltop scene in which the curé expresses his deep love for his parishioners and his intense suffering from the rejection of that Christ-like love: he felt that they nailed him to a cross (1061). Bernanos associates the curé with Christ in both hilltop scenes: the first reveals the curé/Christ's suffering, and the second one evokes a glimpse of the new life of the curé/Christ's Resurrection. These passages

---

[45] "Comme le village, ma prière n'a plus de poids" (1209).

[46] "La haute voix du moteur s'élevait sans cesse jusqu'à ne plus donner qu'une seule note, d'une extraordinaire pureté. Elle était comme le chant de la lumière, elle était la lumière même" (1212–13).

[47] Early in the text, the curé de Torcy summarizes the spirit of childhood by quoting the scriptures (Matthew 18:3 and Luke 18:16): "Unless you become like little children, you will never enter the kingdom of God" (1073).

recall Matthew's sermon on the *mount*, which is a reflection of Moses on the *mountain* of the Ten Commandments.

The result of his experience with Olivier, this "moment of glory," is the change not only in the curé's vision of the outside world, but also of himself (1212). The ride with Olivier lifts him up and sweeps him off his "clumsy, heavy feet" (1208). In the final weeks before his death, the curé feels a new life rising in him: it is "a miraculous expectation" that fills him with an almost painful, inexplicable happiness (1222). After praying all night, the curé asks himself: "What morning can be breaking in me? Will God's grace shine on me?"[48] In reflecting on his diagnosis of incurable stomach cancer, the diarist records his desire to see the dawn again, and evokes images that are "luminous and dazzling" in contemplating his imminent death (1239–41). The curé will die watching the dawning of a new and eternal day outside of Dufréty's window. Whereas on the first page of his diary he observes his parish sinking into (nocturnal and spiritual) darkness, his life ends at dawn.

The reflections entered in his diary hours before death reveal that the curé embraces his newly discovered youth, this "gift from God" (1254). He is able to see the face of his youth for the first time: the "forgotten, rediscovered face" of the beginning of his diary is at last revealed as that of his youth (1036 and 1254). Before dying, the curé is at peace with, even celebrates, his *enfance retrouvée*, as he realizes that reconciling with his youth leads to the ultimate reconciliation—accepting his death through God.

Having at last seen his own true face, the curé's thoughts turn to the world around him: he looks upon it with the smile of a child that he now recognizes as his own. While in the beginning of his diary the curé saw a darkened world turning its face away even from his dying (on a cross), he now sees the face of that world so newly transformed that he cannot imagine himself the victim of ill will. He thinks of Christ "on the Cross," who, even in the midst of his agony, found the "perfection of His *Sainte Humanité* and did not consider Himself the victim of injustice" (1255). The curé describes Christ's pardon (transcribed this time in Latin) as words that have meaning for the youngest child, and thus in facing his own death, he realizes that he must become as a little child in order to "open his eyes to death with child-like simplicity" (1256).

Before the Olivier episode, the curé records an important supernatural experience that also concerns the spirit of childhood. Torcy tells his young friend that the perfect image of the child is that of the Virgin, who embodies innocence and purity: the eyes of the *Vierge-Enfant* are the "only true child-eyes to see our shame and sorrow" (1194). The confirmation of Torcy's

---

[48] "Quel jour va se lever en moi? Dieu me fait-il grâce?" (1223).

words comes to the curé hours later, not as a conscious awareness, but as an experience that takes the form of a vision.

Returning home from his rounds, the curé is overcome by exhaustion and an uncontrollable bout of pain. On a muddy footpath near the home of Séraphita (whose absences from catechism class he hoped to discuss with her parents), he struggles to stay upright, but feels himself sliding into semi-consciousness; then he faints and manages to get up, but without regaining full awareness. At this point, visions of the *Vierge-Enfant* begin to appear to him, and in taking the hand of the "sublime" being—"a child's hand, a child of the poor, already rough from scrubbing" (1197)—the curé perceives her *regard d'enfant*. After stumbling around and falling again, he opens his eyes to see the reflection of Séraphita's lantern that has been placed close to his head (at first the curé thinks this source of light is the rising sun). Séraphita, the curé's "little Samaritan," has found him on the ground, and, taking pity on him, she wipes the vomited blood from his face and offers to help him find his way home (1200). The "refreshing water" on the rag with which she helps to ease his pain announces the curé's feeling overcome by graceful "waters that freshen [his] spirit" just before dying (1255). He then beholds the *regard d'enfant* of his vision in observing the purity of Séraphita's face after she has performed her act of kindness (1200).[49]

Just as the curé brings together the motifs of childhood and poverty in his description of the *Vierge-Enfant*, he links the two motifs in facing his own death: the spirit of poverty and the spirit of childhood are "really one and the same thing" (1246). Throughout his diary the curé chronicles his daily experience of material poverty, which he also confronts in his poor parishioners (with the exception of the countess's family). He even records his lack of confidence in his priestly abilities under the image of poverty, depicting himself as a "pitiful beggar, going from door to door with outstretched hand, not daring to knock" (1141). An important experience of his "miserable childhood"—reading a book by Maxim Gorky—allows the curé to identify with the suffering of the Russian poor (1056). This literary text, unnamed in the curé's diary, is presumably *My Childhood*, in which the author recounts his poor childhood in Tsarist Russia. Reading this book allows the future curé to feel a fraternal love for all *misérables*. In writing about this experience, the diarist adds a religious dimension to his reading of the book by concluding that the poor and suffering find consolation "on the shoulder of Jesus" (1071).[50]

---

[49] The harsh words of Séraphita's father—"Where are you, little bitch!"—interrupt this moving exchange between the curé and the young girl (1201).

[50] Another important experience occurs the night before the curé's death: he meets Dufréty's companion, a woman who incarnates the spirit of poverty. Like the curé himself (and Christ), she shares the burden of the poor.

In discussing poverty with his young friend, Torcy asserts that Christ is its "exemplary figure" (1068). While poverty cannot be taught to the rich, Torcy claims, the love of poverty must be taught to the poor because their special mission is to "represent Jesus' poverty" (1075). The curé de Torcy asserts that to be poor means more than lacking material wealth; it is to embrace the spirit of poverty with the "trust of a child in God's paternal love" (1075). This spiritual point of view transforms the material lack of wealth into a positive religious value—thus the curé d'Ambricourt is poor in spirit.

Poverty is also the subject of one of the curé's discussions with Dr. Delbende, who utters bitter comments on established religion (he has lost his faith and no longer believes in God) to denounce the church's "alliance with the rich" (1095). To Dr. Delbende's rant against the church for not providing the poor with a kingdom in this world, the curé responds (in writing) that the "kingdom of God is not of this world" (1104). Earlier in the diary, he emphasized Christ's eternal presence among the poor as their source of salvation: "There is peace only [in] Jesus."[51]

The significance of the link between the motifs of poverty and childhood hinges on the fact that the curé does not realize that his status as poor man and as child in spirit reveals his own sanctity as well as his association with Christ. The curé then resembles (the image of) the shepherd, about which he writes on the opening page of his diary.

After reconciling with his childhood, the curé becomes reconciled with himself by contemplating his diagnosis and preparing for his own death.[52] He no longer writes about his failure as a priest or the absence of God. After months of spiritual and physical anguish, the curé finds lasting peace in writing these words: "As soon as our Lord appears before me...may His eyes put me at rest."[53] In the penultimate paragraph of his journal, the diarist accepts himself and his death: "The strange mistrust I had of myself, of my own being, is gone, I believe, forever. That struggle is over...I am reconciled to myself, to the poor shell of me."[54] Though in an earlier passage the curé

---

[51] "Il n'est de paix que Jésus-Christ" (1096).

[52] The curé is given his fatal diagnosis by a doctor in Lille in the last part of the novel. Bernanos reverses the narrative order in the beginning of this part: the diarist records his experience of what occurred after leaving the doctor's home before giving an account of his visit to the doctor. (Since he misreads the telephone directory, the curé visits Doctor La*ville* instead of Professor La*vigne*. Thus he leaves the country to die in the city.)

[53] "Que le premier regard du Seigneur...soit un regard qui rasssure!" (1256).

[54] "L'espèce de méfiance que j'avais de moi, de ma personne, vient de se dissiper, je crois, pour toujours. Cette lutte a pris fin...je suis réconcilié avec moi-même, avec cette pauvre dépouille" (1258).

recorded his fear of death in relation to his illness, now his sense of peace in recognizing his "true destiny" removes that fear and puts him at ease (1254).

In reconciling with himself, the curé's last written words indicate that he has indeed found the "supreme grace," which is the humble love of self "as one would love any one of those who themselves have suffered and loved in Jesus" (1258). The reader can then link these words with the curé's first written words, *ma paroisse*. At the end of his life the curé puts his trust entirely in God—"because human agony is above all an act of love (*car l'agonie humaine est d'abord un acte d'amour*)"—acknowledging that God may wish his death as "some form of example to others" (1256). The curé not only accepts himself, he also makes peace with his death in accepting it as God's will. (In addition, he makes peace with the place where he dies, Dufréty's apartment, in which he recognizes the misery of his childhood.) Finally, it is important to stress that the curé is not solely preoccupied with his own death in the final pages of the novel: he still thinks of "looking after" his parish (1255).

Dufréty's letter to the curé de Torcy recounts the final moments of the young curé's life, which include his final words: "'*Qu'est-ce que cela fait? Tout est grâce*'" (1259).[55] Thus in his last spoken words, which echo the Gospel of John (1:3)—"All things came into being through Him"—the humble curé d'Ambricourt accepts his death as a sign of divine grace. Clearly Bernanos illustrates the Christian message of salvation through the death of the curé, who abandons himself to the "gentle mercy of God" to enter "the world of grace" (1139 and 1230). His last words stand in counterpoint to the hatred and sin of his parishioners who, for the most part, rejected him. They also represent a benediction both of his parish and his vocation.

Throughout his diary the curé's vision is identified with that of Christ, though he often fails to realize it. He follows Christ's example by partaking in human suffering and accepting the responsibility for the souls of his parishioners, bearing their agony as would Christ, and urging them to accept salvation. In addition to his Christ-like quality of vicarious suffering, the curé knows the conditions of Christ's poverty and the spirit of childhood from within. His conversation with Torcy (which takes place in the cabin after the countess's death) contains the critical realization that he participates in Christ's suffering as *prisonnier de la Sainte Agonie*: "In truth my place for all time has been the Garden of Olives.... Isn't it enough that today our Lord should have granted me, through the words of my old teacher, the revelation

---

[55] "'What does it matter? All is grace.'" These words come from Sainte Thérèse de Lisieux. Bernanos borrows other expressions from her: the curé compares himself to a "grain of the glowing dust of divine charity," and at the end of his life he claims to have succeeded only "in little things (*petites choses*)" (1113 and 1254).

that I am never to be torn from that eternal place chosen for me—that I am prisoner of the *Sainte Agonie*?"[56] Thus the curé dies for his parish, and all of humanity, by uniting himself with the Passion of Christ.

As the vehicle through which he tries to understand himself, his mission, and his relationship with God, the diary chronicles the spiritual significance of the curé's life, of which he is not fully aware. Although he partially grasps the supernatural meaning of his priestly work, evident in his own reflections on the countess episode, and apparent to the reader in his ability to detect the depths of others' despair before assuming their spiritual suffering, the curé fails to recognize his advance toward sanctity. Bernanos and the reader know that he is a saintly figure, but the humble curé never realizes this fact. Furthermore, the reader can distinguish between the novelist and the diarist in that s/he finds symbolism that extends beyond the curé's written account of events. The curé explains his diet of bread and wine as the result of his poor health, whereas the reader sees the Eucharist. Séraphita's gesture of wiping the curé's face recalls Veronica helping Christ. When the countess declares (before the moment of conversion) that she will surrender only to the curé, the diarist declares that he is "too insignificant": "It's as though you were to put a gold coin in a pierced hand" (1163). Thus, although the curé remains unaware of these Christ-like parallels, for him *tout est grâce*.

---

[56] "La vérité est que depuis toujours c'est au jardin des Oliviers que je me retrouve.... N'est-ce pas assez que Notre-Seigneur m'ait fait cette grâce de me révéler aujourd'hui, par la bouche de mon vieux maître, que rien ne m'arracherait à la place choisie pour moi de toute éternité, que j'étais prisonnier de la Sainte Agonie?" (1187).

CHAPTER 2
The Hero's Inner Drama in Bresson's
Journal d'un curé de campagne

The universality of narrative, as stressed in Roland Barthes' form of structural analysis, embraces both literature and film, given that narrative is comprised of a series of linked events and a set of characters who influence, and are influenced by, those events.[1] Theoretical work in narratology then demonstrates that narrative, as a means of organizing information, is not specific to any one medium. Narrative elements not only exist in both literary and filmic texts, they can also be transferred from the page to the screen.

The means by which narrative is displayed and organized, however, differ from one medium to the other since each has its own properties and conventions. Literary expression entails writing, whereas filmic expression consists of five tracks—moving photographic images, recorded phonetic sound, recorded noises, recorded musical sound, and writing. A novel is adapted to the screen when a filmmaker transforms the literary text using the techniques that define the cinematic medium: s/he employs what Christian Metz calls "specific cinematic codes," those that are unique to cinema, as well as "non-specific codes," those that cinema shares with the other arts.[2]

In adaptation, the filmmaker inevitably has to rework his/her source material because cinema draws on visual, aural, and verbal signifiers, whereas the novel relies on a purely verbal sign system. The reader, for example, employs his/her imaginative ability to visualize a verbally constructed character or setting, whereas the spectator is instantaneously presented the likeness of a specific person or setting on the screen. Furthermore, intrinsic differences exist in the modes and contexts of perception involved in reading a novel and viewing/hearing/reading a film. In general, a novel is read by a reader who is usually alone, at more than one sitting. On the other hand, a film is viewed by a spectator, usually as part of an audience, at one sitting. Under these circumstances, the spectator's emotional contact with the film is continuous.

In "Pour un cinéma impur: défense de l'adaptation," André Bazin views the material, technical, and aesthetic differences between the two media as a challenge to filmmakers that encourages growth in the art of cinema: film can

---

[1] Roland Barthes, "Introduction à l'analyse structurale des récits," *Communications* 8 (1966), p. 7.

[2] Christian Metz, *Langage et cinéma* (Paris: Larousse, 1971), p. 70.

continue to enrich itself by adapting literary texts.[3] In opting for an "impure cinema," he argues against the theorists for whom the highest artistic use of the cinema is to utilize only what other arts cannot, to literally *faire du cinéma*. Finding (creative) filmic equivalents in order to remain faithful to the spirit of the literary text means discovering new cinematic possibilities: adaptation, then, is a question of respect, rather than betrayal.[4] For Bazin, Bresson's cinematic forms of expression in *Journal d'un curé de campagne* provide the paramount example.

Bazin's comments call to mind the vexing question of fidelity to a literary source, which is often posited as a means to judge the success of a cinematic adaptation. Fidelity critics are concerned with how faithful an adaptation is to its literary source, whether or not the film "violates" or "betrays" the source. Yet it is important to recognize that the differing conditions within which literary and filmic narratives are situated render a "violation" of the original text inevitable. Furthermore, the notion of fidelity is problematic because the comparison of a cinematic adaptation with its literary source often implies the superiority of the novel over the film: the spectator expects the film to measure up to his/her own understanding of the original text.

The fidelity issue overlooks the possibility of viewing cinematic adaptations as intertextual works and as critical interpretations of the literary texts, which then enhances and expands our reading of the literary texts. However literal the adaptation, the film represents the filmmaker's subjective interpretation of the literary source. The cinematic adaptation of a novel therefore need not be considered a question of "violating" the source material; rather it is, to an extent that will presumably vary from work to work, a matter of the filmmaker creating an independent, though related, work of art. Placing emphasis on the interpretive nature of adaptation can be an alternative to pure fidelity criticism: instead of judging cinematic adaptations in terms of their faithfulness to the original work or labeling either work as better than the other, they can be viewed as new acts of creativity, coherent and convincing narratives in their own right.

These considerations do not exist in a kind of historical vacuum; to the contrary, they are central to post-World War II criticism about French cinema. The question of fidelity is at the heart of two important articles that appeared in the *Cahiers du cinéma* in the early 1950s. In his celebrated essay about Bresson's *Journal d'un curé de campagne*, Bazin again praises the

---

[3] André Bazin, *Qu'est-ce que le cinéma?* (Paris: Cerf, 1975), p. 95. Bazin is credited with establishing almost single-handedly the study of film as an accepted intellectual pursuit. His impact on the world of cinema is considered greater than that of many filmmakers, actors, and producers.

[4] Ibid., p. 95.

film by describing it as *une dialectique entre le cinéma et la littérature*.[5] Bresson's film marks a "new stage" in cinematic adaptation, in contrast to most post-Occupation cinema: for Bazin it is a "new aesthetic creation, the novel *multiplié* by the cinema."[6] The essay ends with a remark that significantly minimizes the future importance of scriptwriters Jean Aurenche and Pierre Bost, whose adaptation of *Journal d'un curé de campagne* was rejected by Bernanos himself in 1947.

Bazin's essay serves as a precursor to François Truffaut's "Une certaine tendance du cinéma français" (1954), in which Bazin's disciple pays further tribute to Bresson's film.[7] Truffaut's article is a violent attack on the French film establishment of the time—the mainstream quality films, also known as the *cinéma de papa*—and in particular on its leading scriptwriters, Aurenche and Bost. Truffaut sets up an opposition between a *cinéma de scénaristes* (found in quality films) and a *cinéma d'auteurs* (found in Bresson's film) to show that Aurenche and Bost's literary adaptations hinder the realization of the latter, a personal cinema led by directors rather than scriptwriters.[8] In Truffaut's argument, the "scriptwriters' films" do not fully explore cinematic possibilities, and in addition, they demonstrate total irreverence toward their literary sources.

Truffaut's landmark article is in fact a plea for a personal approach to filmmaking (preparing the way for the later arrival of the *Nouvelle Vague*): cinema should be a medium of personal expression for the director who is the *auteur*.[9] Here Truffaut posits his notion of the *politique des auteurs*; the assertion that film directors were artists or *auteurs* just as novelists, poets, painters, and composers were artists.[10] Hence this "policy" concerns the expression of the individual artist—Truffaut sought to reform the French cinema by establishing a cinema of *auteurs*, calling for a specifically

---

[5] André Bazin, "Le *Journal d'un curé de campagne* et la stylistique de Robert Bresson," *Cahiers du cinéma* 3 (June 1951), p. 19.

[6] Ibid., p. 19.

[7] Bazin, the co-founder and central personality of the *Cahiers du cinéma*, guided a group of young critics and future filmmakers including François Truffaut, Claude Chabrol, Jean-Luc Godard, and Jacques Rivette.

[8] Aurenche and Bost's adaptations include *La Symphonie pastorale* (Jean Delannoy, 1946), *Le Diable au corps* (Claude Autant-Lara, 1947), and *Le Rouge et le noir* (Autant-Lara, 1954).

[9] The idea of "auteurism" was first presented by Alexandre Astruc in 1948: his essay "Naissance d'une nouvelle avant-garde: la caméra-stylo" (published in *L'Écran français*) contains his famous declaration about the director's camera being a means of expression just as personal as the writer's pen.

[10] John Hess offers an alternative viewpoint in describing this "policy" as a "justification, couched in aesthetic terms, of a culturally conservative, politically reactionary attempt to remove film from the realm of social and political concern," in "*La Politique des auteurs*, Part One: World View as Aesthetic," *Jump Cut* 1 (May–June 1974), p. 19.

cinematic *écriture*. By increasing the director's creative role, directing becomes an act of "writing" rather than merely following the script as written by the scriptwriter. Aurenche and Bost's scriptwriting then opposes the creative, individualistic work of an *auteur*.

Bresson's film plays a crucial role in the development of a *politique des auteurs* as Truffaut conceives it. Three years after the appearance of "Une certaine tendance," Bresson asserted on the very pages of *Cahiers du cinéma* that "cinema is not *un spectacle*, rather it is *une écriture*."[11] Three decades later, months before the release of his last film, Bresson used the phrase *l'écriture de l'avenir* in reference to cinematic writing: once again in the pages of *Cahiers* he speculated that "with the disappearance of great poets and novelists, *l'écriture cinématographique* will revive writing."[12] Clearly Bresson is one of the few filmmakers for whom the word *auteur* is most suitable, as the majority of contemporary critics praises his personal style of filmmaking, and cites his now famous definition of the *cinématographe* as "a writing with images in movement and sounds."[13]

An important focus of Truffaut's article concerns how Aurenche and Bost changed the tone and meaning of *Journal d'un curé de campagne* by perverting the literary source. Truffaut specifically lashes out against the blasphemous nature of their scriptwriting in two examples. First, Aurenche and Bost alter the scene of the curé's confrontation with Chantal to show her spitting out the consecrated host, which the curé then consumes. Secondly, the proposed script ends with the sacristan's despondent words, *quand on est mort, tout est mort*, whereas the novel ends with the curé's uplifting and spiritual words, *tout est grâce* (1182 and 1259).

Bernanos himself was so offended by Aurenche and Bost's script that he denounced it in a letter published in the newspaper *Samedi-soir* in November of 1947. In addition to the fact that the script ended with the sacristan's "desparaging words," Bernanos also noted his discontent for Aurenche and Bost's elimination of several essential characters (the curé de Torcy, Dr. Delbende, Olivier, and Dr. Laville) as well as for the increased importance given to a very minor character (young Sulpice Mitonnet) so that the curé could be "suspected of pederasty."[14] Bernanos rejected another script that year, written by Father Raymond Bruckberger, a Dominican priest (who worked on Bresson's first feature film). According to Albert Béguin,

[11] Robert Bresson, "Propos," *Cahiers du cinéma* 75 (October 1957), p. 3.

[12] Robert Bresson, interview with Serge Daney in *Cahiers du cinéma* 22 (March 1982), p. 7.

[13] Bresson underlines the importance of this definition in that it appears in capital letters: "LE CINÉMATOGRAPHE EST UNE ÉCRITURE AVEC DES IMAGES EN MOUVEMENT ET DES SONS," in his *Notes sur le cinématographe* (Paris: Gallimard, 1975), p. 18.

[14] Excerpts of Bernanos' letter are quoted by Michel Estève in *Robert Bresson* (Paris: Seghers, 1962), p. 20.

Bernanos' editor and literary executor, this script proved to be one more "failure" because the adaptor transferred the story to the era of the Occupation, thus incorporating a noticeable political slant.[15]

In 1948, producer Pierre Gérin asked Bresson to adapt the popular modern classic. According to Bresson, his own screenplay, which he described as "extremely close to the book," was misunderstood by Gérin.[16] Bresson shot *Journal* in 1950, preferring to change producers (to Union Général Cinématographique) rather than scripts.[17] It is important to point out that Bresson never met Bernanos, who died in 1948. Though the filmmaker said he might have taken more liberties with his script if had he known Bernanos, his guiding notion in adapting *Journal* was "fidelity to the spirit of the literary text by respecting its construction."[18] In Joseph Cunneen's formulation, "fidelity to the spirit of Bernanos' novel meant centering everything on the evolution of the priest's inner life."[19]

The Curé's Aural and Written Narration

Bresson takes the title of Bernanos' novel very seriously, the *Journal d'un curé de campagne*. In the opening shots of the film, a close-up of the curé's first diary entry establishes an important correlation: the literary text of his diary produces the visual text of his life. Bresson also presents a close-up of the young curé wiping his brow, suggesting the physical and spiritual suffering that he will write about throughout the film. The diary and the sweaty face are two expressions of the same anguish. As well as calling attention to the material presence of the diary throughout the film, Bresson emphasizes the curé's act of writing it so that the viewer is continuously reminded of this action, through which the curé emerges as the narrating presence. In order to reinforce the predominance of the diarist's first-person narration, the act of recording entries is repeatedly accompanied by his reading of the entries aloud.

---

[15] Albert Béguin, "L'Adaptation du *Journal d'un curé de campagne*," *Glanes* 18 (May 1951), p. 25.

[16] Robert Bresson, interview with Yvonne Baby in *Le Monde*, November 11, 1971.

[17] The shooting took place from February to April of 1950 in the village of Equirre in the Pas-de-Calais region. Bresson referred to filming *Journal*, which marks a rare occurrence of comments about shoots, in his *Notes sur le cinématographe* (p. 30).

[18] Robert Bresson, interview with Napoléon Murat in *Le Figaro littéraire*, March 16, 1967. Bresson's comment then resembles Bernanos' (implied) definition of adaptation: "the filmmaker has to dream once more the novelist's dream in regard to the spirit [of the literary text]," in Estève's *Robert Bresson*, p. 20.

[19] Joseph Cunneen, *Robert Bresson: A Spiritual Style in Film* (New York: Continuum, 2003), p. 52.

In foregrounding the curé's act of writing and his voice-over narration, Bresson achieves what P. Adams Sitney labels the "equation of narration and protagonist."[20] The curé's verbal commentary not only organizes and guides the filmic narrative; it also replaces dialogue as the primary means of telling the story. The prevalence of the curé's two forms of narration throughout the film, which is highlighted in the chart that follows, underlines the curé-diarist's subjective perspective and restricted interpretation of events. Bresson exploits the curé's act of narrating to accentuate the importance not of the events themselves, but of the curé's vision of the events.

With the exception of two sentences invented by Bresson in section 7, all of the curé's narration comes directly from, or less frequently is based on, the pages of Bernanos' novel.[21] The page numbers found in parentheses on my chart distinguish between passages that are *taken from* the Pléiade edition of the novel and those that are *based on* the literary text; the latter passages contain Bresson's modifications. In the novel, for example, the curé records his uncertainty about Dufréty's desire to see Torcy (1257). In the curé's final written narration on screen, however, he scribbles these words: "He has agreed to meet the curé de Torcy, my old teacher" (section 27).[22] Yet most of Bresson's revisions of the literary text reveal his method of paring down the source: he abridges nearly all of the curé's commentary by eliminating words, sentences, and entire paragraphs.[23]

The chart that follows represents my own analysis. The process by which I acquired the data included several steps: watching the entire film as well as selected scenes (in particular those that contain the curé's narration), reading the novel, listening to the film while searching for the corresponding passages in the literary text, and pausing the images (on close-ups of the diary entries). I performed these steps over and over again to record all the instances of the curé's narration in the film, which I then divided into three

---

[20] P. Adams Sitney, "The Rhetoric of Robert Bresson," in *Robert Bresson*, James Quandt, ed. (Toronto: Cinémathèque Ontario, 1998), p. 129.

[21] Sections are groupings of scenes separated by fades-to-black. Bresson's film contains twenty-seven of them.

[22] In other examples, Bresson changes parishioners' names, turns statements into questions, transforms questions into statements, alters verb tenses, and attributes actions performed by a certain character to the curé or to another character (sections 2, 6, 7, 9, and 10).

[23] In three instances, Bresson abridges the curé's verbal commentary to omit a phrase from the literary text because it is "explained" visually: we *see* the curé running to the chateau, washing his cassock, and holding his hat in sections 20, 21, and 25. (In section 21, the curé's voice-over omits the phrase *six heures et demie*, which is already written on the diary page: Bresson shows a clock to indicate the time.) The filmmaker also cuts out lines relating to the diarist's physical state that are not "explained" visually. In section 13, for example, he omits a sentence about the curé's trembling while writing in his diary (found on page 1125) from the voice-over because the hero does not tremble on screen.

parts: the first column of my chart concerns the curé's aural narration (his voice-over commentary), the second, his written narration (close-ups of his dairy entries as well as any writing that the curé reads in the film), and the third, the act of writing (close-ups of his hand performing that action as well as medium shots in which the curé writes at a table). The chart shows important features of the curé's extensive narration in the film: the aural and written forms occur simultaneously or independently, Bresson displaces or reverses the order of recorded entries as they appear in the novel, and he merges passages from various parts of the literary text into the filmic diary entries.

The Curé's Narration in Bresson's *Journal* - Figure 1

VOICE-OVER NARRATION	WRITTEN NARRATION	ACT OF WRITING
SECTION 1 1. One sentence about writing his diary (taken from page 1036)	Entire entry transcribed	a. Shot of the curé's hand, opens the *cahier* and removes the blotter b. Close-up of the entry already written on the page
2. One phrase about his parish (based on page 1052)	No written narration	No act of writing
3. One sentence about his bad health (taken from page 1141)	Entire entry transcribed	a. Close-up of the page on which the curé writes the entry b. The words *nos joies* (1051) legible above the entry
4. One sentence about the utility of his bicycle (based on page 1053)	Most of entry transcribed	Dissolve to a close-up of another diary page on which the curé writes (above, crossed-out words)
5. Four sentences about his diet (taken from pages 1091, 1105, and 1091)	No written narration	No act of writing
SECTION 2 1. One sentence about Fabregars' visit (based on page 1037)	Most of entry transcribed	Close-up of the page on which the curé writes the entry (above, a crossed-out line)
2. Two sentences about Torcy (taken from page 1036)	No written narration	No act of writing
SECTION 3 1. Two sentences about Torcy, followed by one sentence about the deputy-mayor (based on pages 1039 and 1047)	No written narration	No act of writing

VOICE-OVER NARRATION	WRITTEN NARRATION	ACT OF WRITING
SECTION 3 2. Three sentences about the deputy-mayor (taken from page 1047)	No written narration	No act of writing
SECTION 4 1. One phrase and one sentence about his spiritual crisis (taken from page 1099)	No written narration	No act of writing
[Dissolve]		
2. One sentence about his spiritual crisis (taken from page 1100)	No written narration	No act of writing
SECTION 5 1. One sentence about his catechism class (taken from page 1050)	Most of entry transcribed	a. Shot of the curé's hand, opens the *cahier* and flips through pages b. Close-up of the page on which the curé writes the entry (above, a crossed-out line)
2. One sentence about his students and Séraphita in particular (taken from page 1051)	No written narration	No act of writing
3. Three sentences about his students (taken from page 1051)	Entire entry transcribed	Close-up of the page on which the curé writes the entry (above, a crossed-out line)
SECTION 6 1. Four sentences about Mlle. Louise (taken from pages 1053, 1049, and 1057)	No written narration	No act of writing
2. Two sentences about going to the chateau to see the count (taken from pages 1058 and 1060)	Most of entry transcribed	Close-up of the page on which the curé writes the entry

VOICE-OVER NARRATION	WRITTEN NARRATION	ACT OF WRITING
SECTION 6 3. Two sentences about the count (taken from page 1064)	Entire entry transcribed	a. Close-up of the page on which the curé writes the entry b. Medium shot of him sitting at the table, puts down his pen and inserts the blotter into his *cahier*
4. Three sentences about his diet (taken from pages 1063)	No written narration	No act of writing
5. Two sentences and one phrase about Mlle. Louise and the count (based on page 1065)	Entire entry transcribed	Close-up of the page on which the curé writes the entry
SECTION 7 1. Two sentences about going to the chateau (taken from pages 1145 and 1109)	No written narration	No act of writing
2. One sentence about the servant (taken from page 1145)	No written narration	No act of writing
3. Three sentences about the countess (the first two taken from page 1109, and the third invented by Bresson)	No written narration	No act of writing
4. One sentence about the countess (invented by Bresson)	No written narration	No act of writing
5. One sentence about the countess (based on page 1145)	No written narration	No act of writing
6. Two sentences about his fatigue (based on page 1109)	No written narration	No act of writing
SECTION 8 1. Two sentences about his health (taken from page 1090)	Most of entry transcribed	Close-up of the page on which the curé writes the entry (above, a crossed-out passage)
2. Four sentences about Dr. Delbende (taken from page 1091)	No written narration	No act of writing

VOICE-OVER NARRATION	WRITTEN NARRATION	ACT OF WRITING
SECTION 8 3. One sentence about Dr. Delbende (taken from page 1092)	No written narration	No act of writing
4. One sentence about detecting Dr. Delbende's suffering (taken from page 1096)	No written narration	No act of writing
SECTION 9 1. Two sentences about Séraphita (taken from page 1107)	Entire entry transcribed	a. Shot of the curé's hand, opens the *cahier*, flips through pages and removes the blotter b. Close-up of the page on which the curé writes the entry (above, a crossed-out passage)
2. One sentence about returning her *cartable* (based on page 1107)	No written narration	No act of writing
SECTION 10 1. Two sentences about his struggle to pray (based on page 1110)	Entire entry transcribed	Close-up of the page on which the curé writes the entry (above, a crossed-out line)
2. Two sentences about meeting Torcy and returning home (taken from page 1101)	No written narration	No act of writing
SECTION 11 1. One phrase and one sentence about his nocturnal visit to the church (taken from page 1103)	No written narration	No act of writing
2. One sentence about his spiritual crisis (taken from page 1111)	No written narration	No act of writing

VOICE-OVER NARRATION	WRITTEN NARRATION	ACT OF WRITING
SECTION 12 1. Four sentences about the anonymous letter, three of which contain its transcription (taken from page 1100)	a. Close-up of the prayer (from the Gospel of John) written by Mlle. Louise b. Close-up of the anonymous letter, transcribed in its entirety	No act of writing
2. Two sentences about Mlle. Louise's handwriting (taken from page 1117)	No written narration	No act of writing
SECTION 13 1. Seven sentences and two phrases about his spiritual crisis (taken from pages 1111, 1140, and 1111)	No written narration	No act of writing
2. One sentence about his spiritual crisis (based on page 1125)	Most of entry transcribed	a. Close-up of the page on which the curé writes the entry (above, a crossed-out line) b. Medium shot of him writing at the table
3. Two sentences about his spiritual crisis (taken from page 1113)	Entire entry transcribed	a. Shot of the curé, dips his pen in the ink before recording this entry on the same page as the previous entry b. Close-up of the page on which he writes
4. Three sentences and two phrases about his spiritual crisis (taken from page 1113)	No written narration	Medium shot of the curé, dips his pen in the ink and writes at the table
5. Two sentences about his spiritual crisis (taken from page 1140)	No written narration	No act of writing

VOICE-OVER NARRATION	WRITTEN NARRATION	ACT OF WRITING
SECTION 14 1. Two sentences about his health (taken from page 1118)	Entire entry transcribed	a. Shot of the curé, opens the *cahier* to find a blank page b. Dissolve to a close-up of his hand, finishes writing the entry (above, a crossed-out line)
SECTION 15 No voice-over narration	No written narration	No act of writing
SECTION 16 1. Three sentences about Dr. Delbende's suicide (based on page 1118)	No written narration	No act of writing
2. Three sentences about his own suffering in relation to Dr. Delbende's death (taken from page 1121)	No written narration	No act of writing
SECTION 17 1. Three sentences about his faith (taken from page 1126)	No written narration	No act of writing
2. One sentence about his impression of being called (taken from page 1140)	No written narration	No act of writing
3. One sentence about finding no one there (taken from page 1140)	No written narration	No act of writing
SECTION 18 1. Three sentences about his failure as a priest (taken from page 1130)	No written narration	No act of writing
2. One sentence about going to see Torcy (taken from page 1130)	No written narration	No act of writing
3. One sentence about Torcy's absence (taken from page 1131)	No written narration	No act of writing

VOICE-OVER NARRATION	WRITTEN NARRATION	ACT OF WRITING
SECTION 19		
1. One sentence about reading into Chantal's soul (taken from page 1136)	No written narration	No act of writing
2. Two sentences about his self-confidence (taken from page 1137)	No written narration	No act of writing
3. Two sentences about Chantal's letter (taken from page 1137)	No written narration	No act of writing
4. One sentence about burning the letter, and six sentences about his priestly abilities (taken from pages 1144, 1141, 1160, 1138, 1141, and 1146)	The words *à mon père* legible on Chantal's letter as it burns	No act of writing
SECTION 20		
1. Two sentences about his struggle during the countess episode (taken from page 1157)	No written narration	No act of writing
2. One sentence about reading Dr. Delbende's gaze (taken from page 1162)	No written narration	No act of writing
SECTION 21		
1. One sentence about returning home (taken from pages 1164–65)	No written narration	No act of writing
2. Three sentences about the package delivered by Clovis, and three paragraphs containing the transcription of the countess's letter (taken from pages 1165–66)	Close-up of the first paragraph of the letter	No act of writing
3. One sentence about the countess's death (taken from page 1166)	Entire entry transcribed, as well as one phrase (indicating the time of the countess's death) not given in the voice-over	a. Shot of the ink well on the table b. Close-up of the entry already written on the page (above, a crossed-out line)

VOICE-OVER NARRATION	WRITTEN NARRATION	ACT OF WRITING
SECTION 21		
4. Two sentences about arriving at the chateau (taken from page 1167, and based on page 1166)	No written narration	No act of writing
5. Three sentences about blessing the countess (taken from page 1167)	No written narration	No act of writing
6. One sentence about leaving the chateau (taken from page 1168)	Entire entry transcribed	Close-up of the page on which the curé writes the entry (above, a crossed-out line)
7. Three sentences about returning to the chateau and wanting to spend the night there (based on page 1169, and taken from page 1168)	No written narration	No act of writing
8. Two sentences about entering the countess's room for the last time (taken from page 1169)	No written narration	No act of writing
9. Three sentences about the countess episode and his spiritual strength (taken from pages 1170 and 1169, and based on page 1170)	No written narration	No act of writing
10. One sentence about hearing others whispering as he leaves the chateau (taken from page 1170)	No written narration	No act of writing
SECTION 22		
1. No voice-over narration in the first scene of this section (the curé's encounter with the Canon de la Motte-Beuvron)	No written narration	Medium shot of paper, pen, and ink on the table, but the curé does not perform the act of writing
2. Five sentences about going to the chateau and being greeted by Chantal (based on page 1177)	No written narration	No act of writing

VOICE-OVER NARRATION	WRITTEN NARRATION	ACT OF WRITING
SECTION 22 3. Two sentences about the count's arrival (taken from page 1179)	No written narration	No act of writing
4. One sentence about the countess's burial (based on page 1170)	No written narration	Medium shot of the curé writing at the table
5. Four sentences about the countess episode (taken from page 1184)	One fragment and one complete sentence of the entry transcribed	a. Shot of the curé, dips his pen in the ink and resumes writing b. Close-up of the page on which the curé writes the fragment and the sentence, then underlines the word *sûrement*
6. One long sentence about his thoughts concerning suicide (taken from pages 1184–85)	One fragment of the entry transcribed	a. Close-up of the *cahier*; the curé flips through pages with crossed-out passages, one of which contains the words *en relisant la lettre de Mme la comtesse* (1184), rips them out, and crosses out lines b. Shot of the curé, dips his pen in the ink and resumes writing c. Close-up of the page on which he writes the fragment: unable to complete the word *de*, he drops his pen
SECTION 23 1. Four sentences about being prisoner of the *Sainte Agonie* (taken from page 1187)	No written narration	No act of writing
2. One sentence about his refusal to share the countess's letter with Torcy, and one sentence about returning to the rectory (taken from page 1189)	No written narration	No act of writing

VOICE-OVER NARRATION	WRITTEN NARRATION	ACT OF WRITING
SECTION 23		
[Dissolve]		
3. Seven sentences about reactions to the countess episode (taken from page 1189)	No written narration	No act of writing
4. Two sentences about a future *malheur* (taken from page 1190)	No written narration	No act of writing
5. Two sentences about his ability to take on his vocation (taken from page 1190)	No written narration	No act of writing
6. Three sentences about saying farewell to Torcy (taken from page 1191)	No written narration	No act of writing
SECTION 24		
1. Two sentences about his health in regard to visiting his parishioners (taken from pages 1196–97)	Close-up of the list of parishioners' names written in the curé's *carnet*	Close-up of the curé's hand, crosses out the name Delphanque (listed above Séraphita's) already written in his *carnet*
2. Thirteen sentences about his vision of the *Vierge-Enfant* (taken from pages 1197, 1198, and 1197)	No written narration	No act of writing
SECTION 25		
1. Three sentences about his health and his decision to see the doctor in Lille (taken from page 1201)	No written narration	No act of writing
2. One sentence about waking at dawn (taken from page 1201)	Entire entry transcribed	Close-up of the page on which the curé writes the entry (above, crossed-out lines)

VOICE-OVER NARRATION	WRITTEN NARRATION	ACT OF WRITING
SECTION 25		
3. Two sentences and one phrase about having another hemorrhage (taken from page 1209)	Most of entry transcribed	a. Dissolve to a close-up of another page on which the curé writes b. The words *retenait mon attention* (1209) legible above the entry
4. Three sentences about praying better (taken from page 1208)	Entire entry transcribed	a. Medium shot of the curé writing in a *cahier* on his bed b. Close-up of the page on which the curé writes in pencil
5. No voice-over narration in the final scene of this section (the curé's last encounter with Chantal)	No written narration	No act of writing
SECTION 26		
1. Three sentences about youth (taken from page 1211)	No written narration	No act of writing
2. One sentence about God's desire for him to experience youth (taken from pages 1211–12)	No written narration	No act of writing
3. No voice-over narration in the final scene of this section (the dialogue between the curé and Olivier at the train station)	No written narration	No act of writing
SECTION 27		
1. One sentence about entering a church, and two sentences about his revolt against prayer (taken from page 1228)	No written narration	No act of writing
2. One sentence about staying calm (taken from page 1230)	No written narration	Medium shot of the curé sitting at the café table with his pen in hand (before the voice-over)

VOICE-OVER NARRATION	WRITTEN NARRATION	ACT OF WRITING
SECTION 27 3. Two phrases about cancer and four sentences about his fatal diagnosis (taken from page 1240)	One complete sentence and one fragment of the entry transcribed; another fragment of the entry transcribed	a. Medium shot of the curé, dips his pen in the ink and writes at the café table b. Close-up of the page on which he writes part of the entry c. Medium shot of him writing at the table, then a close-up of him writing d. Medium shot of him writing at the table
4. Three sentences about sitting alone at the café (taken from page 1231)	No written narration	No act of writing
5. One sentence about his urgent need to write (taken from page 1231)	No written narration	Medium shot of the curé, dips his pen in the ink and begins to write
6. One sentence about the mornings at dawn (taken from page 1231)	Entire entry transcribed	a. Close-up of the page on which he writes b. The words *personnes de mon âge* (1240) legible above the entry
7. Two sentences about his shame in returning to Ambricourt with this *chose* (taken from page 1244)	No written narration	No act of writing
8. Two sentences about Dufréty (taken from pages 1057 and 1088)	No written narration	No act of writing
9. One sentence about Dufréty (taken from page 1243)	No written narration	No act of writing
10. No voice-over narration	*Il accepte de rencontrer M. le curé de Torcy, mon vieux maître* (based on page 1257)	a. Close-up of the page on which he writes in pencil b. Medium shot of the curé, writes in pencil (on the bed), drops the *cahier*, then the pencil, and attempts to pick them up

Relations between Narration and Narrative Images

The curé's narration encompasses multiple functions. It can echo, duplicate, or negate the visual rendering of a described episode, act as a transition between scenes or sections (even continuing over dissolves), and the doubling of aural and written narration can replace enactment altogether. When the curé speaks about or records what we are about to see, his narration serves to introduce subsequent images, providing an interpretative frame for them. On the other hand, his verbal commentary can also describe what we have already seen. In this case the curé aurally "replays" a scene to emphasize for the spectator information s/he already knows. The curé's narration can even triple an action in that the viewer experiences the same event through the spoken word, the written word, and in the visual rendering. Finally, the verbal narration can provide the spectator with information about the curé's spiritual development that is not revealed in the visual depiction.

The opening credits of the film appear over the image of the curé's closed *cahier d'écolier*. Next, we see his hand open the notebook and remove a blotter. The camera moves in slowly to a close-up of the page on which the curé has written: "I don't think I'm wrong in jotting down, day by day, without hiding anything, the very humble, insignificant secrets of a very ordinary life" (1036). The curé then reads these lines aloud. Thus Bresson presents the curé's first-person narration from the very beginning of the film to draw (even limit) the spectator's attention to the curé's act of recording: the film will be a projection of what he writes in his diary.

The effect of the opening scene continues throughout the film with repeated shots of the curé recording entries in his beloved pages. We watch him dip his pen in ink, hesitate in recording, rip out pages, blot them, and cross out lines. Ink and paper can be likened to wine and bread as they, too, sustain the curé, while the frequent blotting and ripping reflect his physical and mental anguish.[24] This act of writing becomes dramatic action through which the curé expresses his spiritual meditations, thoughts, and emotions. Bresson told Charles Samuels that the shots in which we see the curé writing show "the contact between his soul and, if you like, the world of matter."[25] In his final diary entry, the only one not accompanied by voice-over narration, the curé's fatigued hand moves slowly across the page, but the diarist is unable to complete the sentence: the end of writing—and the absence of voice-over—prefigures the end of his life.

The filmic narrative is punctuated by images of the curé's journal; shots of diary entries in close-up, of the diary itself, and of the curé's hand

---

[24] The cover image of the Criterion Collection *Diary of a Country Priest* DVD shows an ink splotch and an overturned bottle of ink (Janus Films, 2004).

[25] Charles Samuels, *Encountering Directors* (New York: Capricorn, 1972), p. 64.

recording the entries.[26] The visual depiction of his narrating function is also found in the recurring image of the curé sitting alone at a table recording entries, which reveals the private nature of his writing. In only one scene another character, the café owner (Madame Duplouy of the novel), sees him writing in his diary. When the curé refuses to write an account of the conversion scene for the Canon (as in the novel), he rejects the idea of performing the act of writing in front of another person.

It is important to stress that in the novel we read the completed version of the curé's text, while the filmic diary is linked to process—we witness the diarist's continuous process of recording entries. For example, the act of writing, calling attention to the curé's mediation of events, introduces and concludes the visual representation of the catechism class in section 5. In the beginning of this section, the curé writes lines in which he sets up an expectation about preparing the children for Holy Communion. The action of writing then dissolves to the image of girls entering the church. Next, the curé's voice-over, in which he explains that the girls, especially Séraphita, give him some hope, overlaps with the image of Séraphita and the other girls seated in class.[27] In this scene only Séraphita offers correct (even flawless) responses, yet when the curé keeps her after class to praise her efforts, she mocks him and runs out of the room to join the other students whose laughter indicates that they have conspired against him. This mockery intensifies his spiritual struggle, as does his futile effort (according to Torcy) to be loved by his parish.

The scene ends with a dissolve and resumes the image of the act of writing. This diary entry contains the curé's reaction to the event: he realizes that the girls had planned the joke together, and asks himself why they are so hostile and what he has done to them. Here the curé's narration (both aural and written) replaces the more conventional reaction shot since he verbally expresses his reaction/emotion. Often Bresson does not conventionally depict the curé's reactions in the action of the film; instead the filmmaker employs the visual representation of a diary entry.

While in the novel the curé records recalled events (so that a temporal gap exists between the moment of writing and the past experience to which the entry refers), the curé's act of recording and the experience he has recorded occur almost concurrently on screen. In an important example, we see the image of the diary page on which the curé has recorded the countess's death. We then hear the curé blow out his candle and walk away as the ink

---

[26] When shots of diary entries are separated by dissolves or fades, these punctuation marks suggest a passage of time between two acts of writing.

[27] In the novel, the curé also writes about the boys in the class, who are not to blame if "their precocious realization of sex is now supplemented by weekly cinema" (1051). This passage marks Bernanos' only reference to cinema in the novel.

dries on the page (section 21). Vincent Amiel accurately describes this scene: "we are in the time of the body, not that of remembrance."[28] Later in the film, as the curé sits in the café in Lille trying to make sense of his fatal diagnosis, we watch him write in his journal (section 27). In voice-over the curé explains that he nodded off for a moment as we watch him lean back and close his eyes. A dissolve then reveals the curé's startled face and we hear him say: "Oh God, I have to write it down" (1231). As the curé leans over his pages once again, we realize he is writing what we have just seen and heard. Dudley Andrews refers to this scene as a "daring layering of all three modes of perception, concentrating our imagination with [that of the curé]."[29]

On screen, the curé is not telling his story long after the fact, but reading his story to the viewer as he writes it; the diarist is literally in the process of writing. Noël Burch and Geneviève Sellier refer to Bresson's *rigeur narrative*, given that he does not place the spectator in a more comfortable position than that of the protagonist.[30] The spectator's participation in the act of reading along with the curé provides an example of the "equality" shared by the viewer and the curé. Together with the curé, for example, we compare the handwriting of the anonymous epistle with that of the prayer copied down by Mlle. Louise to discover that she is the author of the malicious note (section 12). We also read the words *à mon père* written by Chantal (on the letter as it burns in the fire), the list of parishioners' names in the curé's *carnet*, and the plaques that hang next to the door of the doctor and of Dufréty (sections 12, 19, 24, and 27).[31] The spectator's act of reading then extends beyond viewing the pages of the curé's diary (filmed by Bresson, for the most part, in close-ups). The question of readership changes from the page to the screen: Bresson's curé never mentions a "future reader" because the spectator assumes that role. The curé shares his pages with the viewer, whereas in the novel when he shows Torcy only a few pages of his writing, the diarist tries to pass them off as those of a friend.

The spectator also has (privileged) access to the curé's inner voice, *voix intérieure*, through off-screen narration. We hear the curé's voice-over

---

[28] Vincent Amiel, *Le Corps au cinéma* (Paris: Presses Universitaires de France, 1998), p. 43.

[29] Dudley Andrews, "Desperation and Meditation: Bresson's *Diary of a Country Priest*," in *Modern European Filmmakers and the Art of Adaptation*, Andrew Horton, ed. (New York: Unger, 1981), p. 29.

[30] Noël Burch and Geneviève Sellier, *La Drôle de guerre des sexes du cinéma français 1930–1956* (Paris: Éditions Nathan, 1996), p. 285.

[31] Bresson invents Mlle. Louise's prayer and the sign next to the doctor's door. In the novel, the curé refers to the list of parishioners without giving their names (1196), discovers Mlle. Louise's address inscribed on a page of her prayer book (1117), sees the words *A Dieu* on Chantal's letter (1144), and visits Doctor Laville not Professor Lavigne (1231). The professional details given on the plaque outside Dufréty's door in the film come from his *carte de visite* and the heading of his letter to Torcy in the novel (1243 and 1258).

narration, both in scenes presenting him alone and with other characters, in every section of the film except section 15. Thus the diary is represented in dramatically depicted scenes that do not contain images of the act of writing. In most of these instances, the diary and the curé's face are linked by off-screen narration. Images of the curé's face are an important visual motif in the film, further connecting the viewer to his inner voice. (The first time we hear voice-over narration, without a shot of the curé writing its corresponding diary entry, the camera dollies forward to frame his face in close-up: the voice-over then motivates camera movement throughout the film.) The curé's off-screen narration serves as a substitute for an action by describing one that is not shown, or doubles an action by presenting commentary as that action progresses or after it has been completed. In the latter case, the curé's voice-over explains the significance, from his perspective, of what we have viewed and heard. The curé's spoken commentary—aural representations of diary entries—also interrupts narrative events. Through these means, Bresson places the action of the film in the perspective of the curé's narration.

(Throughout the film Bresson places the camera in the spatial domain of the hero, signifying the curé's first-person perspective. Yet three times in the film the spectator sees and/or hears what the curé does not. At the end of the countess episode, we observe Chantal outside the chateau, listening under the window. In the novel, there is no equivalent to this shot of Chantal, even though the curé writes two brief descriptions of the grounds outside the chateau from his vantage point inside the *triste salon* during the conversion scene. In both the novel and the film, the curé learns about Chantal's presence from Torcy. In the two other instances, the viewer sees other characters observing the curé: Chantal watches the curé cross the grounds of the chateau before his first encounter with the count in section 6, and Mlle. Louise and the count watch the curé approaching the chateau before his first meeting with the countess in section 7.)

The voice-over narration often provides the spectator access to information about a state of mind or an action that is not visually depicted on screen, even when the curé's narration and its enactment refer to the same event.[32] The sections that contain the curé's religious reflections and his devotion to spiritual concerns reveal the most significant type of scene in which the narration supplies information that Bresson omits from the visual rendering. In section 13, Bresson offers an extended passage of voice-over narration in which the curé describes his attempts to pray. This narration

---

[32] On occasion a discrepancy exists between what the curé says and what we see. For example, in section 6 the count's facial expression does not change even though the curé's voice-over commentary explains that his face hardened. Here the spectator has to depend on the narration in order to interpret the count's behavior from the curé's perspective.

conveys a different view than what is depicted visually since the images of the curé's face and body fail to reflect the full anguish of his thoughts. For example, we do not see the curé tremble when he states in voice-over that something "has suddenly snapped" in his chest, causing him to "quiver for more than an hour" (1125). As the curé records this entry describing his spiritual struggle, Bresson presents a medium shot of the diarist calmly writing at his table.

The visual rendering also excludes the *geste de l'acceptation* described in the voice-over concerning the curé's attempted contact with God in section 13—we only see the curé lifting himself off the floor (using the bed as a crutch) after having performed the gesture. Thus the curé's narration more completely describes his spiritual crisis than does its visual representation: we rely on the narration, rather than the visual rendering, for a more complete depiction of the curé's anguish and his sense of God's silence.[33] Throughout the film the spectator depends on the curé's voice-over narration for access to the diarist's inner thoughts and reactions concerning his spiritual struggle, to his interiority.

Bresson often employs voice-over narration instead of presenting a visual rendering of certain passages of the literary text. In an important example, while we hear the curé's voice-over narration detailing his vision of the *Vierge-Enfant* in section 24, the camera remains focused on the curé's face, entranced, as he stumbles on a muddy footpath. The curé's subjective description of his vision is not visually rendered in the film. As an alternative, the images concentrate on the curé's behavior: we watch him walk in a state of delirium. We hear the rich metaphorical language of the literary text in the curé's commentary, but Bresson does not transpose this language into images. Instead he chooses to employ a high camera angle (to show the curé's opaque face), a tracking camera that moves with the curé, and music to evoke his intense spiritual experience.

Bresson also abridges depicted events so that the curé's verbal commentary conveys only what is of interest to the diarist. For example, in the dialogue between the curé and the deputy-mayor, Bresson shortens the conversation (and refuses to present a complete rendering of the encounter) in order to emphasize the curé's voice-over narration (section 3).[34] The verbal commentary does not relate to their conversation about electricity being installed in the rectory; instead the curé is concerned with the deputy-mayor's role as manager of the village dances (where young men get the

---

[33] This notion also applies to voice-overs relating to God that do not reflect the curé's spiritual crisis. In section 25, for example, he announces in off-screen narration that he is able to "pray better" (1209), yet we do not see him praying.

[34] The scene with Fabregars, the brusque parishioner who exploits the curé's naivete to strike a bargain on his wife's burial, provides another example in section 2.

village girls drunk).[35] With the completion of the shortened dialogue, the diary entry, presented in the form of voice-over narration, gives the curé's interior reaction to the encounter. This scene stresses the curé's role as coordinator of the narrative: his thoughts direct the narrative by introducing the subsequent shot in which villagers (leaving a dance) make noise under the curé's window.

The most remarkable relationship between voice-over narration and images is found in Bresson's double presentation of the diary: we see the curé write lines and hear him read those lines. The image of what he writes in his diary and the sound of his voice-over narration therefore "say" the same thing. (The chart indicates twenty-four examples; in sections 1 and 21 the entry has already been written on the diary page.) In such cases, the narration replaces the dramatization of the described experience because the doubling of the written and aural forms of narration produces autonomous passages.

Just as the voice-over narration often doubles the written entries, it can also double the visual rendering. For instance, as the curé's voice-over explains that he took his lantern to go to the church in the middle of the night, we watch the curé perform these actions in section 11. (The viewer can then relate these actions to his spiritual struggle given that the curé's gesture of blowing out the lantern/flame accompanies his commentary about the absence of God in an earlier scene, thus linking together these scenes with the opening shots of the film in which the curé opens the rectory door to reveal complete darkness.) This kind of doubling of the action, when the curé's verbal narration describes the actions that we witness, marks another "exact" correspondence between sound and image. It occurs in twenty of the twenty-six sections that contain the curé's narration. Once again it confirms the importance of the diary: the recurring verbal narration does not come from an omniscient authorial presence, but from the curé's pen, and by extension, from his voice-overs. It also intensifies the significance of the curé's words about his spiritual crisis and inner struggle. The doubling of sound and image then calls attention to the curé's inner life.

Bresson intersperses the curé's commentary throughout dialogue scenes (as does Bernanos) in order to place those scenes in the context of the curé's *voix intérieure*. It is important to point out that on occasion this voice actually covers up the voices of other characters. The curé withdraws into himself while his voice-over dominates, even replaces, all other sounds. Close-up shots of the curé's face accompany his voice-over narration as it conceals other characters' words in four dialogue scenes (with the deputy-

---

[35] In voice-over the curé reveals that he did not dare talk to the deputy-mayor about the dances. In section 6, when the count brings the curé a rabbit, the voice-over (again) reveals that he does not dare tell the count about his illness, which prevents him from eating anything other than bread.

mayor, the countess, and Torcy in sections 3, 7, 16, and 20). Since the curé's voice-over narration drowns out the other characters' words, his private meditations take precedence over the visual depiction of the scene. In the conversion episode, after the curé's voice-over covers the countess's words, she abruptly asks him: "Have you heard what I was saying?" (1158). The spectator has heard his *voix intérieure*, the voice of the diary, as described by Joseph Cunneen: "leaving ordinary duration, for a brief time we enter the realm of inner consciousness."[36]

The curé's voice-over also interrupts dialogue scenes, such as the critical conversation with Torcy that takes place in the cabin (section 23). As Torcy talks about the vocation of priesthood, the camera slowly moves in to frame the curé's face, after which Torcy abruptly asks him: "What's the matter? Are you crying?" (1187). The curé's voice-over then tells us that he did not realize he was crying, as the camera fixes its place on his face.[37] Next, we see him wipe away the tears as the voice-over resumes: "In truth my place for all time has been the Garden of Olives.... Suddenly our Lord granted me the grace of letting me know, through the words of my old teacher, that I was the prisoner of the *Sainte Agonie*" (1187). When their dialogue begins again, we hear natural sounds from the *monde visible*, the barking of dogs and the bells of a herd of sheep. Bresson adds the latter sound, recalling the literary passage in which the curé compares his suffering parish to a flock in search of a shepherd (1031). The combination of the close-up of the curé's face (image) and his inner voice (sound) allows the spectator to have "contact" with the curé's interiority. His spiritual connection with God is felt, not seen: his voice-over—whose source is, of course, the diary—plays a stronger role in conveying the narrative than does the visual rendering.

Deletions

Bresson connects the material presence of the diary with its spiritual contents: "through the curé's pen, an external world becomes an internal one and takes on a spiritual coloration."[38] In concentrating on the curé's spiritual development, Bresson prunes back other parts of the novel that do not focus on it. The filmmaker decreases the importance of other characters' roles to focus on the struggle within the soul of the hero—the entire film hinges upon his inner life and agony, from his doubts and trials to his understanding and acceptance of his role as "prisoner of the *Sainte Agonie*" (section 23).

---

[36] Cunneen, *Robert Bresson: A Spiritual Style in Film*, p. 46.

[37] In the novel, the curé acknowledges his tears before Torcy asks him why he is crying (1187).

[38] Robert Bresson, interview with Napoléon Murat in *Le Figaro littéraire*, March 16, 1967. This connection between the material and the spiritual recalls the motorcycle scene in the novel: the literary passage marks the progression from the material (the sound of the engine) to the spiritual (the mystical dimension of pure light).

Bresson removes what does not relate, directly or indirectly, to this critical realization, and practically every scene in the film, however insignificant, leads up to it. As the filmmaker himself explained in discussing *Journal*, he strove to "eliminate anything which may distract from the interior drama... the cinema is an exploration within."[39] Bazin reiterated this notion: "for the first time, the cinema offers us a film in which the only perceptible movements are those of the life of the spirit."[40]

In focusing on the curé's *aventure spirituelle*, Bresson stresses the hero's solitude to convey his spiritual loneliness, marked by the absence of God and of a sympathetic community of parishioners. We often encounter scenes of the curé alone—trapped by interiors or alienated in landscapes. The rare establishing shots in the film show him as a tiny figure on the expansive grounds of the chateau, suggesting his solitude. Bresson presents a long shot of him walking to the chateau early in the film, and running there after the countess's death (sections 6 and 21): he is an isolated figure among towering trees. Even the curé's mentor cannot efface his solitude as the two walk up a hill together to the cabin, but the hero walks back alone.[41]

Bresson may add little to Bernanos, but what he subtracts is especially important. The filmmaker removes the social and political dimensions of the novel, most of the pastoral aspects of the curé's ministry, and much of the sensory detail, reducing the layers of the literary text to concentrate on the hero's inner, spiritual drama. (Nonetheless, it is interesting to note that some of this paring down took place after shooting was completed: Bresson cut approximately one third of his film at the editing stage.) While Bernanos develops a series of relationships between the curé and other characters, the filmmaker chooses to exclude many of the scenes that focus on those relationships, rather than on the curé himself. Bresson eliminates several minor characters, the curé's monthly conference with his colleagues, three of his encounters with Mlle. Louise, his first encounter with the Canon, and three of his encounters with Séraphita and/or her parents. The filmmaker also diminishes the presence of Dr. Lavigne and Dufréty. Bresson presents the important diagnosis scene with the former in elliptical fashion—the scene begins with the curé standing in front of the doctor's door and then cuts to a shot of him exiting the doctor's home. As for Dufréty, Bresson excises the

---

[39] Jean Douchet, "Bresson on location," *Sequence* 13 (January 1951), p. 8.

[40] Bazin, "Le *Journal d'un curé de campagne* et la stylistique de Robert Bresson," p. 15.

[41] During periods of spiritual crisis, Bresson emphasizes the curé's loneliness by eliminating his contact with others in the form of dialogue. He also modifies the literary text to stress the curé's solitude: in the novel, the curé and the sacristan (together) beat the dust out of the altar hangings (1181), but we watch the curé perform this task alone on screen (section 22). The Olivier episode marks a rare scene on screen in which we do not sense the curé's solitude: he even smiles during this encounter with a companion his own age.

early setups for this character by omitting his letters. Nevertheless, Bresson
retains many of the central scenes of the novel, such as the curé's encounter
with Dr. Delbende, his "distressing" *rencontre* with Chantal, his
"extraordinary" *rencontre* with the countess, his dialogue with Torcy in the
cabin, his vision of the *Vierge-Enfant* and his subsequent conversation with
Séraphita, his motorcycle ride with Olivier, and his visit to Dufréty.

Bresson adapts the novel not only by thinning out the literary text and
pruning back its elements, but also by condensing scenes. For example, he
combines two of the curé's visits with the countess in section 7, two of his
encounters with the count in section 22, and the curé's two losses of
consciousness in section 25. In addition, Bresson rejects many of the literary
motifs, such as the curé's reflections on poverty and the link between poverty
and childhood, which hinges on the curé's failure to realize that his status as
poor man/child in spirit associates him with Christ. On screen, we *see* the
spirit of childhood in the curé's child-like face and handwriting. We also
witness the curé as a young man full of life riding on the motorcycle in the
Olivier episode. Although Bresson includes in that episode the curé's voice-
over about God's wish for him to "taste the risk of youth" (1211), the
childhood motif is not developed in the film: in the novel, the curé discovers
and acknowledges his *enfance retrouvée*, whereas Bresson chooses to
exclude any voice-over commentary relating the diarist's re-found childhood.

Moreover, the filmmaker eliminates almost all the curé's commentary on
the process of writing (and his problematizing of language), given that only
the curé's first voice-over refers to writing down, "day by day, without
hiding anything, the...insignificant secrets of a very ordinary life" (1036).
The filmic diary is not an object we stumble upon and discover as a finished
product—we mainly *see* the curé write rather than hear or read his comments
about writing, his search for the *mot juste*, and his quest to rejuvenate
language. (Bresson does, however, show the curé's attachment to his pages
by filming a gesture found in the novel: the curé picks up his journal, flips
through the pages, and packs it for his journey to Lille in section 25.) All of
these deletions and abbreviations, which reveal the filmmaker's methods of
reduction and condensation, as well as a genuine shift of emphasis, push the
narrative toward the essential—the curé's inner, spiritual drama.

Dialogue

With one exception, every conversation on screen is a dialogue between
the curé and another character.[42] Throughout these scenes Bresson's camera

---

[42] The conversation between the curé, the count, and Chantal in section 22 is the exception. In
addition, in one instance the curé simply overhears a conversation on the steps of the chateau
(section 21), and in two scenes he does not talk to the other character (Torcy's housekeeper in
section 18 and the café owner in section 27).

repeatedly frames the curé's face when other characters are talking, suggesting the filmmaker's concentration on the diarist's inner reaction to events.[43] According to Bazin, "Bernanos himself would have taken more *libertés* with his book had he been the scriptwriter."[44] While the curé's verbal narration, for the most part, comes directly from the novel, the dialogue scenes show more of Bresson's transformative work, his *libertés*, as he invents several lines of dialogue in numerous scenes of his film—in eighteen of the twenty-eight sections that contain dialogue.[45]

Bresson dramatizes the curé's indirect discourse in many scenes, such as the catechism class, so that lines from the diarist's meditative passages in the literary text about his encounters with other characters become lines of dialogue on screen (in twelve of the twenty-eight sections that contain dialogue).[46] In order to turn the curé's private commentary into dialogue, the filmmaker also invents minor characters, such as the curé's colleague who recounts the circumstances of Dr. Delbende's death in section 18.

While Bresson abbreviates to some extent all of the dialogues in the film, in relation to those that are transcribed by the curé in the novel, he significantly abridges the conversations between the curé and Torcy, Dr. Delbende, the countess, and Dufréty (in sections 2, 8, 16, 20, 26, and 27).[47] Omitting parts of the literary dialogues allows the filmmaker to modify the narrative. For example, during the curé's important confrontation with Chantal in the novel, the adolescent tells him about the affair between her father and Mlle. Louise (1134). In the opening shots of the film, however, Bresson quickly defuses this source of dramatic interest—the curé sees a couple (the count and Mlle. Louise) embracing and catches their averted, suspecting gaze. The guilty response observed in the return gaze of the count and his mistress suggests the curé's ability to look into others' souls. The couple's offended look also implies that the curé is an intruder, an outsider, which characterizes his relationship with most of the parish.

In addition, the filmmaker frequently reverses the order of certain lines of dialogue as they appear in the literary text, as well as the order of entire

---

[43]The camera also lingers on the curé's face following the completion of an important dialogue —after Chantal leaves the church, after Torcy leaves the funeral, and after the count leaves the rectory in sections 16, 19, and 26.

[44] Bazin, "Le *Journal d'un curé de campagne* et la stylistique de Robert Bresson," p. 8.

[45] Bresson often invents lines in order to join two passages of dialogue from the novel, reflecting his method of paring down and condensing the literary text.

[46] It is important to note that Fabregars delivers one of Torcy's lines (section 2), and the countess—not the curé—delivers a line from a meditative passage in the novel (section 7).

[47] Bresson also modifies some of the literary dialogues. For instance, the deputy-mayor's visit to the curé concerns the installation of electricity in the rectory (section 3), whereas the town council agrees to dig a well in the novel (1047).

scenes. For example, Olivier takes the curé to the train station en route to Lille in section 26 of the film. In the novel, however, Olivier drops him off at the rectory; the curé's replacement arrives, the hero reflects on his encounter with Olivier, receives a short letter from the latter, and converses with Chantal before leaving for Lille (1221–27). On screen, Chantal visits the curé at the rectory before his motorcycle ride with Olivier in section 25.[48] Although Bresson reverses the order of dialogue scenes as they appear in the literary text, the spectator (who is not familiar with the novel) does not experience any loss of meaning.

Scenes that feature dialogue between the curé and the countess illustrate several features of Bresson's transformative work. In the novel, the countess performs the cathartic act of recounting her son's death to the curé (1150), whereas early in the film Mlle. Louise tells him about the countess's dead child—in lines invented by Bresson in section 6. As a result, when the curé visits the countess for the first time, she is holding her son's funeral mass card.[49] Bresson then invents their dialogue in the first part of the scene.

The filmmaker further emphasizes the countess's memory of her son in the conversion episode: she frequently turns her back to the curé to look at her child's picture on the mantle, which marks another invention by Bresson (section 20). The filmmaker pares down the dialogue in this episode by excluding elements such as the curé's important phrase *l'enfer c'est de ne plus aimer*, and all of his references to his role as priest/confessor. Bresson also chooses to exclude the diarist's comments about the broken fan because it symbolizes the countess's spiritual struggle, rather than that of the curé. He then alters the curé's voice-over in his subsequent visit to the chateau in section 22: the diarist remarks the presence of the charred logs rather than the broken fan so that the narration doubles the image (we see the logs).

Inner Movements

Bresson criticized the *cinéma* for being "photographed theater," as opposed to his notion of the *cinématographe*, which abolishes all theatrical expression.[50] Related to his rejection of *cinéma* in favor of *cinématographe*, the filmmaker refused the term *acteur* in favor of *modèle*: a painter uses a

---

[48] Bresson also presents the curé's first encounter with Mlle. Louise after the catechism class (sections 5 and 6), his first conversation with the countess after his meeting with Dr. Delbende (sections 7 and 8), and his second dialogue with Torcy after the curé himself (rather than his *enfant de chœur* as in the novel) returns Séraphita's book bag (sections 9 and 10).

[49] We can read this mass card, invented by Bresson, while the curé only sees it in the countess's hand: *Souvenez-vous devant Dieu Jean-Philippe de Saint-Robert rappelé à Dieu le 10 mai 1925.* This is the only complete date given in the film (section 7).

[50] Robert Bresson, "Une mise en scène n'est pas un art," *Cahiers du cinéma* 543 (February 2000), p. 4.

model, not an actor, to make a painting. Starting with *Journal d'un curé de campagne*, Bresson began to suppress dramatic intentions through extremely precise direction of speech, movement, and gesture. When *modèles* are stripped of such intentions, they are forced to reveal themselves—the inner motivations of their words and gestures—through the automatism imposed on them by Bresson. While actors are conscious of playing a part, Bresson's *modèles* do not act.[51] He demanded automatic responses without inflection or emotion, forbidding his *modèles* to expressively interpret the text.[52] Bresson also rejected the traditional process of character building (for the purpose of encouraging spectatorial identification in the theater), and particularly the psychological exploration of character motivation. As he stated in his *Notes sur le cinématographe*, "what the *modèles* show me is not important; rather what they hide from me, what they do not even know exists inside them."[53]

By concentrating on the inner, spiritual adventure in which the curé is engaged, Bresson removes what he considers to be extraneous or false. His method then seeks to reveal the inner life of the curé or what the filmmaker calls "the innermost and imperceptible movements."[54] Not surprisingly, Claude Laydu, the *modèle* who "played the role" of the curé d'Ambricourt, was shocked when he saw the saintly figure he had become on screen.[55]

Laydu's deadpan narration in the film—he delivers words in voice-over and in dialogue with the same flat tone in spite of the often spiritual subject matter of the corresponding diary entries—results from Bresson's ruling out of dramatic expression as well as psychological motivation. While actors are trained to project artificial emotion, Bresson demanded that Laydu speak his lines as if "to himself."[56] Just as he strove to visually neutralize the intentionality of the *modele's* "performance," Bresson also worked to flatten the aural dimension by demanding Laydu's non-expressive monotone delivery. In the words of critic Raymond Durgnat, "the monotone and the deadpan represent not a mask, but a revelation of the essential man."[57]

---

[51] Robert Bresson, *Notes sur le cinématographe*, p. 99.

[52] Roland Monod, "En travaillant avec Robert Bresson," *Cahiers du cinéma* 64 (November 1956), p. 20.

[53] Bresson, *Notes sur le cinématographe*, p. 17.

[54] Robert Bresson, interview with Jacques Doniol-Valcroze and Jean-Luc Godard, *Cahiers du cinéma* 104 (February 1960), p. 6. According to Bresson, his films consist of "inner movements *that can be seen*," in his *Notes sur le cinématographe*, p. 83.

[55]*Dans le film, je n'ai jamais pensé passer pour un personnage mystique, j'ai été...étonné en voyant le film de m'apercevoir que les choses que j'avais essayé de ressentir étaient presque sublimes*, in Robert Droguet's "Robert Bresson," *Premier plan* 42 (November 1966), p. 34.

[56] Bresson, *Notes sur le cinématographe*, p. 84.

[57] Raymond Durgnat, "Le *Journal d'un curé de campagne*," in *The Films of Robert Bresson*, Ian Cameron, ed. (New York: Praeger, 1969), p. 46.

In Bazin's formulation, Bresson concerns himself only with "spiritual reality, the movements of the soul."[58] In his diary, the curé also writes about *les mouvements de l'âme*, revealing a key connection between Bernanos and Bresson (1183). Bazin argues that the countess episode shows Bresson's ability to depict the workings of grace without relying on the psychological and dramatic values of dialogue.[59] It is important to comment on a specific moment in this episode. In the novel, the curé burns himself by reaching into the fire to retrieve the medallion, which allows the countess to transfer her maternal instincts in bandaging his wound. In the film, the curé is not burned. Bresson refuses the sentimentality and concentrates instead on the priest's gesture of digging in the ashes.

Ten years after its release, Bresson stressed the critical role that *Journal* played in consolidating the unique, esoteric style of the *cinématographe*, what he called his "anti-system."[60] Based on *écriture*, this "anti-system" remained almost unchanged in Bresson's *œuvre* after *Journal*, the film in which he determined many of the techniques, such as no acting, no actors, and no studio shooting, he had been seeking to define his *cinématographe*. For the title role Bresson chose Laydu, an unknown and inexperienced stage performer who had never appeared in a film.[61] Only Marie-Monique Arkel, in the role of the countess, and Antoine Balpêtré, in the role of Dr. Delbende, were familiar faces for the spectators of the 1950s.

Sounds: the Texture of the Everyday

Throughout *Journal* Bresson uses expressive sounds as both symbolic and dramatic elements. After Dr. Delbende's funeral, for example, the curé and Torcy have a conversation near the church in which the mass was celebrated (section 16).[62] Torcy tells the young priest about his friend's last years through the window of his car, and each time he finishes a statement, we hear the soft slam of a car door. Then with each reply uttered by the curé, most

---

[58] André Bazin, "*Un condamné à mort s'est échappé*," *France-Observateur* 340 (November 1956), p. 22.

[59] André Bazin, "Le *Journal d'un curé de campagne* et la stylistique de Robert Bresson," p. 16.

[60] Bresson, interview with Napoléon Murat in *Le Figaro littéraire*, March 16, 1967.

[61] According to critics' accounts, Claude Laydu, who was not Catholic, spent time in a monastery to prepare for the film, starved himself during shooting to look sickly, wore a real priest's cassock, and carried Bernanos' novel with him. Nevertheless, Laydu's face does not correspond to the literary description: the curé catches sight of himself in a mirror and observes his "long nose, deep lines descending on either side of his mouth, and bristly chin" (1092).

[62] In the novel, this dialogue takes place on a bench near the train station. Bresson invents several lines of the filmic conversation and turns the curé's indirect discourse into dialogue, drawing from pages 1119–22.

often in the form of a question, we hear the sound of a starting motor. This rhythm is broken when the curé learns that Dr. Delbende killed himself.

The most striking example of Bresson's use of sound occurs in the conversion scene. First, we hear a raking sound as the curé approaches the chateau. We think the sound comes from a gesture performed by the countess: she is raking the coals in the fireplace with a poker when the curé enters the *triste salon*. (The curé does not, however, reflect on the spiritual value of the poker, as in the literary text.) During the pauses in the conversation between the curé and the countess, we hear the raking sound coming from the grounds of the chateau.[63] Here the countess performs a gesture invented by Bresson. She closes the window, presumably to assure their privacy and to block outside noise. (In the novel, the countess stands near the closed window.) But she is in fact closing herself in with the priest, accepting his presence, and we learn that this gesture fails to assure privacy because Chantal overhears their conversation. The final time we hear the raking sound, we at last see the object that has been producing it: the camera leaves the interior of the chateau to show the gardener raking outside.[64] In the novel, the appearance of Clovis the gardener marks the beginning and the end of the countess episode, and the curé sees him during the episode as well, once he has finished his task of chopping wood, not raking. In the film, however, the curé does not see Clovis until after the countess episode.

This mundane sound heightens the contrast between the everyday world and the curé's inner world, his incredible struggle for the redemption of the countess's soul. It reminds us that everyday life continues outside the *triste salon* and offers relief from the spiritual and emotional tension of their dia-logue.[65] In the novel, the curé writes about the calm, familiar sounds he hears coming from the kitchen during the countess episode, sounds that occur in the *monde visible*, to contrast them with the supernatural quality of the conversion scene (1161 and 1169). Bresson replaces the novel's verbal commentary with the raking sound, which has become a famous example of using sound as a counterpoint to action: his soundtrack records the noises of everyday life, of worldly reality, which are counterpoints to the supernatural

---

[63] We hear the sound after the curé tells the countess that he "fears her death" more than his own, after she tells him that she has "too much common sense," after the curé tells her that she is "face to face with Him," and finally, after the countess prays "Thy kingdom come" (1152-63).

[64] Bresson often shows the object from which a sound originates in a later scene (or later in the same scene as with the rake): while we hear the sounds of barking dogs and passing carts in the opening section of the film, we do not see a dog or a cart until section 6.

[65] For Keith Reader, the raking sound is an "echo of the priest's pen moving across the page, a suggestion that what is going on inside the chateau, on the screen, is some kind of raking bare or gathering up of souls," in "The Sacrament of Writing: Robert Bresson's *Journal d'un curé de campagne*," *French Film: Texts and Contexts*, Susan Hayward and Ginette Vincendeau, eds. (New York: Routledge, 1990), p. 143.

drama. Sounds are not treated as mere consequences of visible actions in *Journal*, but stand on their own, carry meaning, add emotional resonance, and replace images.

The Final Image: *Tout est grâce*

In transposing the diary form of Bernanos' novel to the screen, Bresson places the narrative in the context of the curé's verbal commentary. The only time the narrative focus passes from the interior to the exterior occurs at the end of the film. The curé de Torcy narrates the final section by reading aloud Dufréty's letter, which contains his first-hand account of the curé's death. Torcy's reading of the letter is accompanied by the image of a cross, which fills the screen as his voice-over recounts the curé's last moments and words. The close-up of Dufréty's typed letter dissolves into a long fixed shot (lasting ninety seconds) of the shadow of a cross against a pure, white screen.[66]

The images fixed on the curé's face throughout the film announce the final image fixed on the cross. Bresson often focuses the spectator's attention on the curé's face, usually as a complement to his voice-over, to give us access to his interiority: we are able to read the "inner movements" on his face. In the opening shots of the film, as the curé unlaces a package from the back of his bicycle, which presumably holds all of his belongings, he hears a whistling sound, accompanied by the sound of a passing cart; he then turns his head to look in the direction of the sounds he hears. Though the viewer anticipates a depiction of the object(s) of his gaze, the source of the sounds, Bresson refuses to present it, choosing instead to remain on the curé's face. In paying his last respects to the countess, the curé's voice-over speaks of her appearance: "I wanted so much for her to smile—she was not smiling" (section 21). Yet this commentary does not lead to a shot of the countess; instead the camera stays on the curé's face, showing an unreciprocated gaze into off-screen space. In the final shot of the curé, after he struggles to write his last entry (the first one he does not read aloud), the camera moves in to linger on his face in a long take.[67] Bresson refuses to cut to the object of his gaze: the countershot does not materialize. As the curé gazes into off-screen space throughout the film, looking intensely beyond the frame, he may be searching for God: only the curé's faith can fill the void.

The screen turns black after Torcy's voice-over pronounces the curé's final words: *Qu'est-ce que cela fait? Tout est grâce* (1259). These closing

---

[66] The final image is accompanied by music from Jean-Jacques Grunenwald's conventional score, which is heard in twenty of the film's twenty-seven sections, most often in association with the curé's voice-over. Bresson stops the musical accompaniment during three dialogue scenes to highlight the voice-over narration (in sections 8, 23, and 24).

[67] The first time we see the curé on screen, the camera also moves in to frame his face (as he wipes sweat from his brow).

words will resonate with powerful tones in four of Bresson's subsequent films, *Un condamné à mort s'est échappé* (1956), *Procès de Jeanne d'Arc* (1962), *Au hasard Balthazar* (1966), and *Mouchette* (1967). Through the stages of his loneliness and illness, the curé progresses from pain to grace. The filmic diary also chronicles his crisis of faith, which causes him to suffer spiritually, but all of these lead to divine grace. We learn that his first voice-over is incorrect. The curé's life is hardly insignificant or ordinary; rather it is permeated by grace. In his verbal commentary throughout the film, the curé records his incapacity to fulfill his priestly mission, but in God's eyes he has not failed, as expressed in his final words. According to Bazin's formulation, "the film offers a new dramatic form that is specifically religious, or better yet, specifically theological: it is a phenomenology of salvation and grace."[68]

We see crosses in the film before the appearance of the final image.[69] In several instances Bresson films the curé agonizing in his room, and the background is marked by a crucifix that hangs over the bed. The crucifix remains in the shadows, suggesting the curé's spiritual crisis due to God's absence: "There is only a black wall before me...God has withdrawn from me," explains the curé's inner voice (section 13 and page 1111). According to Michel Estève, an expert on both Bernanos and Bresson, the crucifix in his room is "always shot in the shadow because the priest is undergoing the 'dark night' evoked by John of the Cross."[70] The last shot of the film, the shadow of a cross, then marks the inversion of the cross shot in shadow.

The final image of the cross is unique in the film: it is a sign of spiritual transfiguration that confirms the curé's final words and his realization of grace. The final image offers a judgment—the affirmation of the curé's state of grace—that derives from an omniscient or god-like authority. This crucial judgment is not mediated by the curé: Bresson presents his assessment of the curé in that the image reveals authorial perspective. The film recognizes its author just as the curé has acknowledged the grace of God.

Just as the diary is a material object that acquires interior, spiritual value through the curé's reflections in the film, Bresson suggests the progression from the material to the spiritual in its final image—that image acquires its meaning by replacing the physical world. According to Ellen Feldman's formulation, "the physical world is transcended and the image we see does not represent a corporeal reality as do the others in the film."[71] It is important

---

[68] Bazin, "Le *Journal d'un curé de campagne* et la stylistique de Robert Bresson," p. 15.

[69] On four occasions the curé makes the sign of the cross (to perform the final blessing at mass in section 6, to bless the countess in sections 20 and 21, and to bless Torcy in section 23).

[70] Estève, *Robert Bresson*, 34.

[71] Ellen Feldman, "Bresson's Adaptation of Bernanos' *The Diary of a Country Priest*," *West Virginia Philological Papers* 26 (August 1980), p. 42.

to stress that the curé's body, as well as Jesus' body, is absent from the final image. In Raymond Durgnat's formulation, "the spiritual has devoured the flesh."[72] For Paul Schrader, "the priest 'gives up' his body, metamorphosing into the image of the cross."[73]

With the final image, Bresson directly depicts the curé's spiritual reality. The empty cross encapsulates the life of the nameless curé: throughout the film he grows spiritually as the cancer physically diminishes him. It marks the culmination of all that has come before, suggesting the curé's profound suffering and alienation as well as his attainment of grace. The curé's final words, *tout est grâce*, and Bresson's final image of the cross confirm the hero's understanding of his place in the Garden of Olives and his acceptance of his role as *prisonnier de la Sainte Agonie*. Bresson's concentration on the curé's inner, spiritual drama throughout the film culminates in the realization of grace in the final image. The style of the last shot in *Journal*, like much of the film, can be summed up in Bresson's use of absence to create presence.

---

[72] Durgnat, "Le *Journal d'un curé de campagne*," p. 48.

[73] Paul Schrader, *Transcendental Style in Film: Ozu, Bresson, Dreyer* (Los Angeles: University of California Press, 1972), p. 88.

CHAPTER 3
The Heroine's Redemption in Bernanos'
Nouvelle Histoire de Mouchette

Mouchette is a solitary being who inherits misery from a long line of ancestors, like her predecessor the curé d'Ambricourt. She lacks, however, the conceptual and verbal tools for an explicit spiritual consciousness because her experience is limited to the physical. Thus Bernanos not only organizes Mouchette's thoughts and memories to explain the psychological sense of her experiences, he also takes responsibility for her spiritual destiny. Just as the curé assumes the suffering of others, Bernanos takes on his heroine's burden.

Nouvelle Histoire de Mouchette tells the story of the rape of a fourteen-year old girl and her suicide by drowning. The author divides his novel into four parts: each part is progressively shorter and takes place in a different location, reflecting the increasing intensity of Mouchette's story. The first part involves the encounter between the heroine and Arsène the poacher, which results in rape. The second part concerns the heroine's encounter with her mother, which ends in the latter's death. In the third part, Mouchette makes three stops in the village where she meets with the grocer Madame Derain, Mathieu the gamekeeper and his wife, and Philomène, a death-obsessed old woman. All of these *rencontres* signify a series of humiliations for the heroine. Finally, in the fourth part, Mouchette takes her life in an abandoned quarry. The author accompanies his heroine along the course that leads her from the sudden blossoming of love to its transformation into horror and shame. In less than a day, the woods become a labyrinth, her family home a tomb, her love a rape, and her dream a nightmare. Yet in spite of her suicide, Bernanos carries his heroine from rejection to redemption.

The Heroine's Misery

The condition of misery was the author's main preoccupation while writing *Nouvelle Histoire de Mouchette*. Inspired by the atrocities and suffering he witnessed in Majorca during the Spanish civil war, Bernanos hoped to speak for all *misérables* and to praise the dignity with which they endured misery. In an interview with André Rousseaux, literary critic and close friend of the author, Bernanos discussed this historical source of his short novel: in observing truckloads of the Spanish poor on their way to execution, he was struck by "their incapacity to understand the atrocious game in which their lives were engaged."[1]

What do the wartime fate of the Spanish poor and the story of the rape and suicide of a French peasant girl have in common? They share the tragic destiny of being innocent victims of a misfortune, *malheur*, they cannot understand. Bernanos observed human beings who were uncomprending and uncomprended. Mouchette is associated with the Spanish in her own inability to comprehend: though she may fight courageously against it, Mouchette is unable to understand the fated quality of her inherited misery. In the Rousseaux interview, the author stressed the human significance of his literary work, shown in the exemplary dignity of his heroine's resistance to destiny. In place of any notion of a "hopeless case," Bernanos insisted on her noble and heroic character in that her resistance exemplifies "the honor of the poor." In likening Mouchette's death to "that of a bull who, after fighting to the best of his ability, can do nothing more than bow his head"—an echo of Spain—Bernanos asserted that it is not exactly a suicide; rather "she falls asleep after having waited until the very end for help that never came."[2] This interview reveals the author's compassion for Mouchette's innocent suffering and his admiration for her courage in confronting misery.

The novel contains another significant motif that ultimately concerns the dignity of all *misérables*. The author's historical inspiration has to be put in the context of his intention to write a story that would show the "awakening of the sense of purity" in the consciousness of an *enfant misérable*.[3] A close reading of the text confirms the importance of this purity motif, particularly in the context of the rape. Furthermore, it links this Mouchette with the earlier character of the same name in the author's first novel *Sous le soleil de Satan* (1926)—although they are two distinct characters, the second Mouchette comes from the same *monde imaginaire* as the first Mouchette (Germaine Malorthy), who also searched for a sort of authentic purity. Thus the author's two sources of inspiration for *Nouvelle Histoire de Mouchette* include a historical event and a literary project, bringing together the motifs of misery and purity.

Misery is Mouchette's birthright, as she and her family belong to what the author names the *race des misérables* (1340). The heroine does not create her misfortune, as does Germaine Malorthy; rather she is born into it. Her grandfather's sordid existence (tainted with an extreme physical ugliness) captures the tone of the family's poverty, her father's alcoholism and

---

[1] Michel Estève, *Bernanos* (Paris: Gallimard, 1965), p. 243. The Rousseaux interview was originally published as "Misère et grandeur de Mouchette" in *Candide* (June 1937).

[2] All quotations in this paragraph are from the Rousseaux interview in Estève's *Bernanos*, p. 244.

[3] Georges Bernanos, *Correspondance II* (Paris: Plon, 1971), p. 136.

frequent abuse cause the heroine to endure horrible nightmares, her mother's final agony consummates a lifetime of struggle against misery, and her baby brother's howling defines his role as the last-born in a line of alcoholics. Even Mouchette's immediate physical environment is saturated with misery, as the frame of rotten boards of her house is deteriorating. As a result, the heroine is accustomed to feeling cold, which marks a "discomfort like so many others" (1271). Hunger is yet another sign of her misery. On practically every page of the text, she is noticeably "marked by the sacred sign of misery" (1343).

The nature of the heroine's inheritance of misery is found in a precise physical image, her hands. This sign of her own malediction and that of her ancestors inspires disgust in her. When she gazes upon her soiled hand for the last time (and feels detached from her own body), Mouchette notices the "same unlucky kind" of her mother's hands, and her deformed thumb bears a striking resemblance to that of her father—these signs of hereditary weight are the stigma of her birthright (1340). Mouchette inherits her ancestors' misfortune, suffering, and wretched material conditions: this misery is "as impassable as the walls of a prison" (1302).

In the first part of the novel, Bernanos describes the experience of Mouchette, her family, and all *misérables*:

> If the *misérables* could associate the various images of their poverty, they would be overwhelmed by this *malheur*, but their wretchedness seems to them to consist simply of an endless succession of miseries, a series of unfortunate chances. They are like blind men who, with trembling fingers, count out the coins whose value they cannot calculate. For the *misérables*, the idea of poverty is enough. Their *misère* is faceless.[4]

If this misery is "faceless," it is also a condition without boundaries: misery manifests itself in the author's native Artois (where the novel takes place) as well as in Majorca (where Bernanos witnessed the atrocities of the Spanish civil war).

Since the heroine's experience as an *enfant misérable* is confined to the realm of the physical, the reader encounters a lack of contemplation and an absence of spiritual life in the young girl. The author often likens his heroine to an animal (cat, dog, hare, partridge) given that she is a creature of instinct

---

[4] "Si les misérables avaient le pouvoir d'associer entre elles les images de leur malheur, elles auraient tôt fait de l'accabler. Mais leur misère n'est pour eux qu'une infinité de misères, un déroulement de hasards malheureux. Ils ressemblent à des aveugles qui comptent de leurs doigts tremblants des pièces de monnaie dont ils ne connaissent pas l'effigie. Pour les misérables, l'idée de la misère suffit. Leur misère n'a pas de visage" (1270–71).

who lacks reflection. Bernanos emphasizes Mouchette's familiarity with the sounds of nature, and implies that her solitude and isolation are to a certain extent the result of her timidity, which resembles that of wild animals.

During the storm in the first part of the novel, Mouchette races through the woods "like an animal caught in a trap," and in giving up the struggle, she returns to her instinctive animal-like resignation (1270). After the rape, Bernanos depicts his heroine as "a hunted animal," and in the last part, Mouchette again resembles "a trapped animal" (1321 and 1342). It is important, then, to stress the fact that since Mouchette is a creature of instinct likened to an animal, Arsène's role as poacher gains more significance for she becomes his game: "He watches her with a calm and self-possessed scrutiny...the way he examines tracks, which he alone knows, at the edge of the woods."[5]

As a result of her lack of conceptual and verbal sophistication, the heroine perceives the world around her and expresses herself through her senses. For Mouchette, voices, hands, and faces are the primary means of human expression, and the senses of hearing, smell, sight, and touch are the primary vehicles of perception. Throughout the novel, Bernanos emphasizes her heightened senses, which in effect dominate her ability to "feel and think" (1318). Clearly Mouchette's experience is almost entirely limited to her sensations, resulting from an immediate and direct contact with what surrounds her—she only perceives from reality what her senses allow or bring to her.[6]

Bernanos constantly refers to Mouchette's incapacities to emphasize that not only is she guided by her senses and instinct, she is also incapable of understanding her own feelings. After the rape, for instance, the heroine is unable to understand why she hates herself, and although she is the victim, Mouchette cannot hate her aggressor. The heroine is intellectually incapable of comprehending the injustice of her world and emotionally incapable of localizing that injustice in Arsène, so she can only turn her anger inward against herself. What she feels immediately after the rape is not rage against Arsène; rather it is a "pain" she cannot understand (1297). In the last part of the novel the heroine then fails to grasp the true meaning of her encounter with the poacher: she struggles to comprehend or even experience "the

---

[5] "Il l'observe, sans colère, mais avec une attention tranquille...comme il examine à la lisière du bois, une trace connue de lui seul" (1294).

[6] For example, the author emphasizes the importance of sounds to convey his heroine's auditory world. Hearing is her most developed sense, which corresponds to her sensitivity to others' voices (evident in all her encounters and particularly those with Arsène). Through auditory terms and constant references to sound, Bernanos faithfully evokes Mouchette's experience so that the reader enters her world of senses.

emotions that a town girl, with her mind full of serials and films, could feel so easily" (1338).[7]

The Author-Narrator's Voice

Mouchette's incapacity to express or even understand her feelings reveals the importance of the author's narration. In *Nouvelle Histoire de Mouchette*, the diary form is somewhat irrelevant because Mouchette is incapable of conscious reflection. (The narrative perspective also differs from *Sous le soleil de Satan* because the first Mouchette is able to think, act, and reason on her own.) Bernanos employs third-person narration, yet he is able to enter the sensory and instinctive mode of expression that in all probability would come from his heroine if she possessed the faculties of self-expression and introspection. The narrative voice assumes that of the first person, weaving in and out of her thoughts and feelings so that the reader experiences the narrative as if Mouchette herself, like her predecessor the curé, has given voice to the story.

The reader shares Mouchette's experience because the author tells the story through her perceptions and reactions, just as he describes the storm and the landscape through his heroine's senses. By restricting the narrative perspective to Mouchette's point of view, the author takes the risk of placing his reader in a state of incomprehension, like that of Mouchette, or intervening too much on her behalf. Bernanos avoids both risks by employing a narrative style that reveals, as Brian Fitch argues, "the skillful transition between the young peasant girl's perceptions and the author's literary imagination and sensibility."[8] The narration then contains a double voice: Mouchette's voice and that of the author-narrator. The latter contains two temporal dimensions—the present and the interior past of the character. In several passages of the novel, what appears at first to be information supplied by an omniscient narrator is in fact the heroine's memory, *souvenir*. In these cases, the author-narrator explains his heroine's memories of the past, which she is incapable of expressing.

While the author-narrator's presence in the short novel is particularly evident when he offers commentary or openly intercedes on his heroine's behalf, it is in effect a constant presence intervening between the reader and the girl's tragic experience. Bernanos is present to such an extent that Albert Béguin identifies him as an "invisible character."[9] By providing the lucidity

---

[7] Bernanos refers to the cinema a second time when he adopts his heroine's point of view to compare Arsène's face with "those of film stars, which she had sometimes seen in newspapers" (1288).

[8] Brian Fitch, *Dimensions et structures chez Bernanos* (Paris: Lettres Modernes, 1969), p. 157.

[9] Albert Béguin, *Bernanos par lui-même* (Paris: Éditions du Seuil, 1954), p. 80.

that is lacking in Mouchette's inner experience, Bernanos assumes the responsibility of clarifying and even expressing his heroine's thoughts. The following passage illustrates the author's method of conveying her thoughts and the subtlety of his narrative style: "Her clogs have one advantage—if she pushes her toes to the end, treating them like a pair of enormous castanets, she can make a noise that drives *Mme l'institutrice* crazy."[10] This is certainly Mouchette's thought, as she would use the phrase *Mme l'institutrice*. The narrative style then reveals her way of thinking or speaking while going well beyond the power of expression of an "unfortunate child who can hardly formulate even elementary ideas" (1305).

Since Mouchette also lacks the ability to think in a coherent manner, Bernanos puts her thoughts in order for her. Following a passage about her father's alcoholism, written in the form of interior monologue, the author informs the reader that thoughts never pass through Mouchette's mind "in such a logical manner" (1271). Bernanos directly refers to his heroine's incapacity to establish a logical link between her thoughts when she looks at Arsène's body, and again, after organizing Mouchette's thoughts about purity, he informs the reader of her "incapacity to clearly form such thoughts" (1303). Just before her suicide, the author explains once more that his heroine seeks in vain to arrange her disordered thoughts. These interventions are necessary so that the author does not completely substitute himself for Mouchette. In this way, he makes his role as author clear to the reader; Bernanos does not try to erase his own presence in the text. He warns the reader about his heroine's incapacities (as well as the fated quality of her situation), while respecting the nature of her naive consciousness to preserve the authenticity of her experience. In fact, the author's interventions assure his heroine's autonomy.

In addition to these interventions, the author uses interjections to reveal his heroine's thoughts to the reader. This narrative technique allows Bernanos to unite Mouchette's thoughts with his explanation of them, evident in the following passage: "Damn scarf! No, it is not new! Yet it makes the rounds in the family as needed."[11] Here the interjections that come directly from Mouchette's interior monologue are followed by the author-narrator's explanation of the importance of the scarf: the reader imagines the

---

[10] "L'avantage est qu'en s'appliquant à les balancer [ses galoches] au bout des orteils ainsi qu'une paire d'énormes castagnettes, elles font un bruit qui met Mme l'institutrice hors d'elle-même" (1265).

[11] "Maudit fichu! Ce n'est pas un fichu neuf, non! Mais il passe de l'un à l'autre selon les besoins" (1270). Another important example is found on the first page of the novel. Mouchette has removed her clogs in order to run faster; she puts them on again, but on the wrong feet. Bernanos then inserts his heroine's thought/interjection (*Tant pis!*) before explaining that the shoes are too big for her (1265).

beating the heroine would receive for losing the one scarf used by every member of her destitute family. Through Mouchette's exclamations, found in each part of the text, the author-narrator provides the reader direct access to the heroine's thoughts.

At times, Bernanos also avoids naming the heroine's emotions to communicate her limited mental experience. In describing the feeling experienced by Mouchette when looking at Arsène's face, for example, the author-narrator avoids naming her awakening of love and makes it clear that she is incapable of doing so. As Arsène and Mouchette exchange glances, the author-narrator speaks of a "feeling that she cannot name" (1281). This narrative technique allows the author-narrator to preserve the unique character of his heroine's feelings, while once again revealing Mouchette's incapacity to understand or express them.

The presence of the author-narrator gains even more significance in the matter of Mouchette's rescue from misery. The absence of a priest-figure or "Bernanosian saint" in *Nouvelle Histoire de Mouchette* indicates that no character can assure Mouchette's salvation. Bernanos himself then takes on a sacerdotal function in looking upon his heroine with the mercy of God. This notion is evident in the "prayer" of the novel's epigraph, which the author dedicates to both Mouchettes: "May God have mercy on one and on the other!"[12] Albert Béguin argues that Bernanos conveys this vision of mercy through his *style de la tendresse*, which not only reflects the author's compassion for his heroine, but also convinces the reader of her salvation.[13]

A reflection of his concern for the suffering of the Spanish poor, the author's compassionate and sympathetic attitude toward his heroine characterizes this *style de la tendresse*. Of the twelve suicides in his *œuvre*, Bernanos arguably shows the most compassion for Mouchette's fatal act.[14] In fact, he takes on his heroine's burden in *Nouvelle Histoire de Mouchette* by accompanying her along her path of suffering: his compassion for Mouchette signifies (literally) that he suffers with her. Bernanos also requests the reader's compassion for his heroine, as illustrated in these interventions found in the important passage about Mouchette's loss of purity: "O wretched childhood, that does not want to die!.... O ineradicable defilement! (*Ô maudite enfance, qui ne veut pas mourir!.... ô souillure ineffaçable!*)" (1304–05). Here the author-narrator intervenes on his heroine's behalf to engage the reader's sympathy.

---

[12] "A l'une et à l'autre que Dieu fasse miséricorde!" (1263).

[13] Albert Béguin, *Bernanos par lui-même*, p. 80.

[14] The characters who commit suicide are Mouchette in *Sous le soleil de Satan*, Pernichon in *L'Imposture*, Fiodor in *La Joie*, Madame Louise, André, and Evangéline in *Un Crime*, Dr. Delbende in *Journal d'un curé de campagne*, Philippe in *Un mauvais rêve*, Arsène, Eugène, and Hélène Devandomme in *Monsieur Ouine*, and Mouchette in *Nouvelle Histoire de Mouchette*.

He also engages this sympathy by presenting his heroine as an innocent victim, like the Spanish poor: "Her role is simply that of a child who blundered into a mortal struggle between grown men."[15] The heroine is a brutalized and deprived *child*. Nature's storm, the poacher's rape, and the alcoholic father's abuse characterize the violence of her world. This brutality also manifests itself in the indifference of the villagers. The gaze of farmer Ménétrier, the last person who sees Mouchette before she takes her life, summarizes their insensitivity: his look is "as indifferent as that of his horse" (1344). Futhermore, Mouchette is deprived of familial love and affection (evident in that she has no last name): she has never known "the gentleness (*douceur*) of a true caress" (1341). Although the author-narrator evokes her past encounter with a tall fair-haired girl who "gently stroked her cheek" at a *fête*, this *souvenir* only emphasizes the unjust quality of the heroine's existence because she had already learned, at the age of ten, to reject affection (1341).

In addition to his *style de la tendresse*, Bernanos implies, even assures, his heroine's salvation through the symbolic passage from descent to ascension (and from darkness to light). The feeling of ascension at the end of the novel opposes the images of descent in the first parts. In the beginning of the story, Mouchette is situated on the crest of a slope, overlooking the school, which she descends to move toward the woods. During the storm, her foot becomes wedged in the mud and she falls into a ditch. The images of descent reach a climax in her flight from the hut after the rape, as Mouchette slips again and slides down the side of a hill. At the moment of her suicide, however, the heroine enters the water fixing her gaze on "the highest point in the sky" (1345). Moreover, the imagery in *Nouvelle Histoire de Mouchette* evolves from mud to clear water, as the author-narrator emphasizes the purity of the "gentle water" in the final paragraphs. The heroine's death occurs in a place of calm during the daylight hours: as opposed to the violence of the nocturnal landscape, the mud, rain, and squalid interiors of the preceding pages, the placid and pure water of her suicide provides an image of rescue or salvation rather than despair.

Even though the reader of *Nouvelle Histoire de Mouchette* finds no allusion to a God-like presence in the person of a priest-figure, the presence of the divine is constant in Bernanosian fiction—and its interpretation is Christian—whether or not the characters are aware of it. It is important, then, to reiterate Bernanos' conception of his writing as a sacerdotal and spiritual vocation, a priestly calling through which he could contribute to the salvation

---

[15] "Son rôle n'est plus que celui d'un enfant fourvoyé parmi des hommes affrontés dans une lutte mortelle" (1317).

of souls (his readers). In the name of Christian love, the author-narrator seeks his heroine's salvation through God.

Given that Bernanos' religious fiction exposes a continual reflection on the Passion of Christ, the author implicitly presents the death and resurrection of Christ in the life of a girl who is incapable of spiritual consciousness. From a Catholic perspective, Bernanos exposes the Passion hidden in the experience of an *enfant misérable* who does not possess the curé's (devout) insight. Furthermore, the short novel contains no explicit images of Christ, in contrast to the strongly Christocentric *Journal d'un curé de campagne*. The familiar images of God, which permeate Bernanos' other novels, are absent in Mouchette's story because the heroine lacks a spiritual life: the fourteen-year old's world is characterized by both physical and spiritual poverty.

Bernanos does, however, propose the image of a cross, even though it is absent the day of his heroine's suicide. Moments before taking her life, Mouchette looks at the hamlet below from atop an embankment, just as the curé looks upon the village with the feeling that he will be crucified by it. Mouchette, of course, does not think about crucifixion, but Bernanos indicates that the water in which she will die flows through an old quarry where the accumulating waters have worn a grotto in the embankment—the notice at the entrance (warning off trespassers) "casts a shadow like a cross" if seen in the moonlight (1338). With the exception of this description of a cross, the reader does not encounter any explicit Christian references in the novel, as the heroine lives in an indifferent and dechristianized society where "no one goes to High Mass anymore" (1327).

Breaking the Solitude

Throughout Mouchette's story, the author-narrator stresses her isolation from society, the *village détesté* (1281). In the opening pages of the novel, the heroine spies on her teacher and her classmates from outside the school: Madame and her peers represent the indifferent society from which she withdraws herself. Her encounters with others reflect her innocent suffering in a series of rejections that increase her solitude: "She is alone now, completely alone, against everyone."[16] In spite of Mouchette's seclusion from society, one person breaks through the walls of her solitude and even gains her trust. Yet the opportunity for a genuine relationship is destroyed by the violence of rape, as her potential expression of love—hidden deep inside, waiting to be born "like a seed of wheat beneath the snow" (1288)—ends in bitter humiliation.

---

[16] "Elle est seule, vraiment seule aujourd'hui, contre tous" (1317).

Mouchette's encounter with Arsène marks the only time in the narrative (and in her life) that the ordinarily withdrawn girl makes contact with another person to briefly end her isolation from society. In recounting to Mouchette his escapades, describing recollections of his childhood (focusing on an account of a cyclone, which he compares to the present storm), and sharing his bottle, Arsène not only creates a feeling of mutual complicity, he also accords her a status and an acceptance she has never before experienced. The poacher admires her not only for "standing up to a beating" from her father, but also for facing her father while he beats her (1283). In turn *bel Arsène* is someone for whom she can feel admiration—even after the rape (1304).

Furthermore, the poacher confides to Mouchette his greatest secret: he has killed a man. This revelation weakens her walls of defense because when Arsène asks her to act as his alibi in the murder of Mathieu the gamekeeper, the heroine feels overwhelmed by this newfound confidence in her. Mouchette has at last found a companion worthy of her own spirit in that Arsène's defiance of the law in his role as poacher resembles her own rebellion against the villagers. Both Mouchette and Arsène are solitary beings, rejected by the social order incarnate in Madame (schoolteacher) and Mathieu (gamekeeper): they are, in fact, connected by the secret of a murder that symbolizes the death of that social order.

Mouchette hopes and dreams of being connected to her fellow outcast by loving him, though the author-narrator reminds the reader that she remains incapable of understanding her feelings. During the encounter with Arsène, Mouchette's awakening of desire (a new feeling she is incapable of naming) begins with her gaze upon the "first human face" she has ever truly contemplated (1288). This face of her companion in misery is a "mysterious double of her own face" (1289). Mouchette then discovers sexual desire through the contemplation of the Other, though she remains unaware of it: "Her desire, like the warmth of her living body itself, spreads throughout her veins—it is not concentrated in any one precise image."[17] Her pleasure in looking at Arsène's face marks the revelation of her love, another feeling she cannot name: Mouchette remains incapable of understanding what she comes "from the depths of herself," a feeling that is mixed with erotic fascination (1288).

The brutality of rape shatters the heroine's dream of love—she is "duped by a dream" (1311). After having tried to love one person in her detested society, Mouchette's "great hope" becomes her "deception of love" because Arsène betrays this hope (1304 and 1338). The heroine looks for some sort of liberation by loving Arsène, but the person she hopes to love—"the only one

---

[17] "Son désir est comme la chaleur même de son corps vivant, répandu à travers ses veines, et ne se fixe en aucune image précise" (1291).

from whom she would not flee" (1296)—simply inflicts violence upon her.[18] At the end of the novel, Mouchette will seek in death what "love refuses her" in life (1339). The author-narrator will then imply that her death marks an opening toward love, which she does not find on earth.

The heroine's other opportunity to connect with a human being, her mother, is destroyed this time by death. Mouchette's memory of the rape, the only point of impact with reality throughout her nocturnal experience, is so powerful that she wants to divulge her secret. Yet when Mouchette at last feels the courage to blurt out, "Mama, I have to tell you…" her mother dies and her probable confession about the rape remains unheard (1315). This non-revelation, which ends the encounter with her mother, deepens the child's solitude and misery.

In fact, all of Mouchette's encounters with others are incidents in a life comprised of "an infinity of miseries" (1270). After the rape, she experiences several *rencontres* that strip away the pretenses of her dream. Upon discovering that there was no cyclone the night before, her confusion and anguish resulting from this exposure of Arsène's lie (and of her naive acceptance of his tale) compel Mouchette to learn whether the rest of her belief in his love is also false. She then seeks the truth about what happened to her the previous night.

At each stop along the path, her disastrous night with Arsène is revived, and instead of reassuring her that the love she experienced was real, each encounter only confirms that she was deceived by a dream. The villagers spurn and mock her for the very act she had hoped to incarnate as love, as Mathieu's indifference reveals that of society in regard to the rape victim.[19] His lack of concern for Mouchette, whom he addresses as "vermin," is evident: "How is any of this my business? Young hares are my business" (1325). Of course in learning that Mathieu is alive, the heroine discovers Arsène's second lie. This discovery means that she no longer has to protect the man responsible for the imaginary crime, whom only she could save from the law. Like her blossoming love, the false murder is an illusion, a dream.

The Wind and the Imaginary Cyclone

Bernanos introduces the wind motif, which he will use to convey his heroine's dream-like experience, in the opening sentence of the novel: "The

---

[18] Moments before the rape, Mouchette tells Arsène that she would rather kill herself than do anything to harm him (1295). Here she utters simple and naive words that hide unformulated thoughts confirming her destiny.

[19] Two of these encounters, nonetheless, begin with a hint of kindness. Yet the sympathy extended to Mouchette (for her mother's death) by Madame Derain turns to derision when the marks of Arsène's attack show through her torn blouse. While Mathieu's wife shows gentleness toward the girl, Mouchette herself is unable to bear the pity and refuses to be alone with her.

dark west wind—the sea wind as Antoine would say—is already scattering voices in the darkness."[20] Early in the narrative this wind grows more powerful as Mouchette plunges into the forest, and she becomes the victim of its thrashing. Then the dilapidated shack (one of Arsène's hideouts) fails to provide her protection from the blustery weather. The wind's anger also rages in the description of the cyclone that Arsène had witnessed as a youth: he tells Mouchette that the wind "resembled a dragon" (1276). The wind continues to "howl angrily" in the poacher's account of his fight with the gamekeeper (1285). The violence of the wind in Arsène's stories about the cyclone and the "murder" of Mathieu then reflects the violence of his actions: branding his wound, his epileptic fit, and the rape.

When Arsène leaves the shack to look for her lost shoe, Mouchette hears "the last breath of the wind in the tree-tops" (1279). The strong voice of the wind appears to quiet down at last. (The wind continues to blow, but not as aggressively.) Yet Mouchette remains a victim of the wind: its violence is replaced by that of Arsène as the echo of the wind's howl is now heard in Arsene's breathing. In brutally disinfecting his wound (resulting from his fight with Mathieu), the poacher separates the last embers of the fire, picks one out, and "blows on it again and again" (1280). Moments before the rape, Mouchette already feels his breath on her neck, and the rape scene ends with the following description: "There was nothing to be heard in the shadows but the panting breath of *bel Arsène*."[21] The author-narrator depicts Arsène's breath as the human equivalent of the wind so that his *souffle*, like the "wind's mighty anger" (1301), represents a destructive force against Mouchette—it is associated with violence and sexual brutality, becoming the metonymic expression of the rape.

In *Nouvelle Histoire de Mouchette* the wind contributes to Mouchette's dream-like experience, becoming symbolic of her illusion. In her mind the cyclone described by Arsène becomes synonymous with the seasonal rainstorm of that night: she believes that she has actually experienced a cyclone. And further, since Bernanos adopts Mouchette's perspective, so does the reader, to some extent. The heroine transforms the real events of her encounter with Arsène into a dream since the cyclone blows only in her imagination. The conversation with her mother, however, modifies and subverts the nocturnal experience: she explains to Mouchette that the "cyclone" was no more than a "strong sea breeze," and the neighbor did not even remove her sheets from the clothesline (1310). Here Mouchette

---

[20] "Mais déjà le grand vent noir qui vient de l'ouest—le vent des mers, comme dit Antoine— éparpille les voix dans la nuit" (1265). The reader never learns the identity of Antoine, who is most likely one of Mouchette's brothers. Bernanos includes this phrase about him to reveal his heroine's fleeting thought to the reader.

[21] "Il n'y eut plus rien de vivant au fond de l'ombre que le souffle précipité du bel Arsène" (1296).

momentarily awakens from her dream to realize that most of what she experienced was only fantasy.

The total calm of the last part of the novel signifies the end of her illusion, as the air is *immobile* at her suicide (1343). The wind that tyrannized the night—the substance of her illusion—completely disappears when Mouchette reaches the abandoned quarry. From this familiar place, the heroine sees "a thin column of smoke rising toward the sky" (1338). It is important to note the contrast between this column of smoke rising (peacefully) to the sky and the "column of dead leaves" beaten down by the rain and wind in the first part of the text—dead leaves are replaced by smoke in the tranquil atmosphere of the last pages of the novel (1272).[22] If the rising smoke carries the religious symbolism of the elevation of her soul to heaven, it is a sign announcing Mouchette's salvation. Furthermore, it may be an allusion to Able's smoke rising (and Cain's merely smoldering) as well as to the column of smoke preceding the children of Israel en route to the Promised Land.

The Heroine's Song/Purity

While the heroine's refusal to sing with her classmates marks her rebellion against society, it is this same vehicle of song through which she expresses her love to Arsène. In spite of her *voix charmante*, the author-narrator reveals her inexplicable hatred for singing in class, as each note hurts her "to the depths of her soul" (1266). Bernanos describes Mouchette's efforts to avoid singing in terms of a "cruel struggle": her refusal to sing indicates her reluctance to reveal this innermost part of herself (1267). When Madame forces her to sing, Mouchette tries to distort the purity of tone to keep some part of herself from the contamination of others. She purposely sings out of tune in order to hide the purity of her voice, coming from the depths of her being.

However, as Mouchette holds Arsène's head during his epileptic fit, her song comes naturally and spontaneously.[23] She momentarily breaks her self-imposed silence to share with Arsène the only "secret" that she possesses, her beautiful voice (1291). In exchange for his secret of murder she gives him her most cherished one, her song. The *chant* is more than her secret: the author-narrator also reveals its transcendent sense as her gift of self by assimilating the gift of her song with the gift of her body. This "pure voice," which Bernanos likens to snow, symbolizes her purity even though

---

[22] Furthermore, these dead leaves are associated with Arsène in an earlier passage: he can spot his game among them near the woods (1294).

[23] When awakened at night by the noisy return of her inebriated father, Mouchette often hums a familiar tune (heard in the local café) to lull herself back to sleep. With Arsène, she summons the courage to sing aloud this "Negro dance-tune, as they called it" (1291).

Mouchette is incapable of understanding that this "mysterious" voice was in fact the expression of her youth in "its sudden blossoming" (1292). The association of her beautiful voice with her virgin love is not, even intuitively, grasped by Mouchette. The author indicates the purity of this gift, *ce trésor*, in that the child in Mouchette still dominates the woman, and in the comparison of the *chant* to a "spring" (1292). Her clear, pure song is transformed for Mouchette into an inviting water that "refreshes her body and soul," in which she wishes to "immerse her hands" (1292). Bernanos therefore likens Mouchette's song/purity to water, which suggests her eventual drowning and the purification of that act.

Through her song Mouchette temporarily transcends her destitute condition, creating a (single) moment of joy in her life of misery. She gives her love to Arsène as never to anyone else in the society against which she rebels and from which she is so isolated. Bernanos suggests that this gift of self, purity, and love in effect collapses Mouchette's defense against society (1292). But Mouchette sings her song without being heard, recalling her status as an "invisible observer" in the beginning of the novel: her *chant* is offered to "a corpse on the bare ground" because Mouchette sees the epileptic fit as an imitation of death (1290).

Upon regaining consciousness, the poacher's reaction shows his total incomprehension: he demands to know "what in the world" she is singing (1292). Arsène understands nothing of the love the girl is feeling, of its purity or its intent: for him, love is only a physical act. The "sweetness" of Mouchette's song is then transformed into the violence of Arsène's brute force: he seizes her with "violent hands" and hurls her against the wall (1292 and 1296). Arsène answers her gift of love and purity with this act of brutality. Having exposed her gift of self through song, Mouchette is raped and more alone than ever. Her song is then replaced by a "funereal chant," implying an aural suggestion of her death (1301). Furthermore, after offering it to Arsène, her voice loses its purity: she tries to cover up her baby brother's crying with a song that quickly becomes "no more than a discordant wailing" (1311).

Once the poacher has violated the girl's purity, Bernanos stresses Mouchette's lost virginity rather than the absence of love on Arsène's part. At first the heroine experiences a "horrible nausea" (1297). Her pain is certainly physical, though she cannot understand its nature: the author-narrator must explain that her suffering is both physical and moral. Since Mouchette is incapable of formulating the association, the author-narrator links her purity (and youth) with her virginity, and encourages the reader to see the revelation of this purity through its opposition with *souillure* (1303).

Bernanos then associates Mouchette's shame with the loss of her purity/virginity. Hatred for her own body as a result of the rape reveals her humiliation: "Her hands, with no forgiveness in them, remain clenched on the mattress and refuse to touch her hated body."[24] Yet Mouchette remains incapable of understanding that the "shame of her flesh and bones" has its origin in her loss of purity/virginity: "Why? What did she do wrong?" (1320). Furthermore, this loss signifies the "death" of her childhood. During the mother's agony, she addresses her daughter with the name *Doudou*—this nickname represents the heroine's childhood. Thus in dying the mother symbolically takes the child *Doudou* with her. In her mother's arms, Mouchette tries in vain to reclaim her childhood: "For an instant, the stubborn little head resists imperceptibly, and then sinks onto the mother's breast, yielding, as if at the end of its strength, with a weary moan."[25]

The author further develops the purity motif during Mouchette's meeting with Philomène, *la veilleuse des morts* (the protector of the dead), which marks the heroine's last encounter before her death.[26] Philomène speaks to Mouchette only of death and even provides the piece of material, a corpse's dress, which will symbolically become the heroine's shroud. (In the second part of the text, Bernanos likens Mouchette's tattered dress to a "shroud," and she wears a "funeral veil"—1296). During this visit, the heroine sees the "immaculate white sheets" in Philomène's linen closet as a source of "soft, pure light," which she then associates, even confuses, with "the idea of death" (1331). Philomène teaches Mouchette that all living things are dirty by extolling the virtues of death and giving it the allure of purity. Her (profane) lesson prefigures the author-narrator's (spiritual) presentation of Mouchette's suicide as, in part, an act of purification.

Water and Drowning

The element of water dominates Mouchette's world and the author-narrator's numerous references to it foreshadow her death by drowning. This liquid takes on various forms: the heavy rain, the viscous air of Arsène's recalled cyclone, the humidity that invades the family home, and the quarry in which she dies. While water pelts Mouchette in the beginning of the novel, it embraces her in the end, as water imagery progresses from negative

---

[24] "Ses mains ne pardonnent pas, refusent de toucher le corps haï, restent crispés à la paillasse" (1300).

[25] "Un instant, la petite tête obstinée résiste imperceptiblement, puis glisse tout à coup sur la poitrine maternelle, s'abandonne, avec un gémissement de fatigue, et comme au terme de son effort" (1314). This passage recalls Bernanos' comments in which he compared Mouchette's death to that of a defeated bull.

[26] Bernanos devotes four pages to the description of this character whose religion or "mysterious faction" is defined by her adoration of and obsession with the dead (1326–29). Some critics consider her the closest character to a priest-figure in the short novel, yet Philomène represents the villagers' indifference because her main interest in Mouchette is her dead mother.

aspects, such as torrential rain and stagnant ponds, to the clear, pure, and welcoming water of the abandoned quarry. (We have seen that the author-narrator compares Mouchette's *chant* to an alluring water, suggesting the water in which she drowns.) Bernanos constantly presents his heroine in association with water. In the beginning of the novel the "dampness soaks her stockings," and at the end she feels the "gentle sting of the cold water" (1268 and 1345). In stressing the heroine's perpetual contact with water in the first parts of the novel, the author-narrator prepares the reader for her complete immersion at the end.

Bernanos also develops the drowning motif through analogical language and descriptive passages: these figurative references to drowning materialize at the end of the narrative.[27] Metaphors in *Nouvelle Histoire de Mouchette* that reflect the feeling of drowning correspond to the inundation of water in the setting. The heroine feels her heart "submerged in a delectable anguish" while she is spying on her peers, and upon returning home she picks up her baby brother "with a movement as spontaneous as that of a drowning victim" (1267 and 1299). The author-narrator further develops drowning imagery in that the heroine feels "enveloped in silence" upon arriving at Mathieu's house (1326). Then at Philomène's house, Mouchette feels herself drowning in it: "She tries to struggle against this silence…[but] it envelops her, and she feels as if an invisible cloth were covering her shoulders and face."[28] At first, Mouchette tries to resist this feeling, like a drowning victim struggling to keep from going under, but finally succumbs. When she stops resisting the silence, she "slides into it with an almost physical delight" (1330). These passages announce the heroine's suicide because Mouchette "slides into the clear water" in the final paragraph—here the water that flows over her head and neck fills her ears with its "joyous sound" (1345).

The quarry in which Mouchette drowns is subtly foreshadowed by references to springs and clear water. When leaving school, the heroine hears a poplar tree "murmuring like a spring" (1269), her song resembles a "pure, clear spring" (1292), and hearing the word "purity" evokes the image of "clear water" for Mouchette (1303). After failing to confide in her mother, the heroine feels as though "a spring has suddenly dried up" (1330). These

---

[27] Thus Bernanos prepares the reader for the literal drowning through which the second Mouchette finds the peaceful rest that the first Mouchette longed for: in *Sous le soleil de Satan*, Germaine (Mouchette) Malorthy wants to drown herself in a pond. Although Bernanos describes the first Mouchette's "submission to Satan" in terms of drowning (207), it is essential to stress important contrasts between the two suicides: the second Mouchette remains a victim of evil, rather than choosing evil as does the first Mouchette, and she encounters a peaceful death, as opposed to Germaine's horrible slitting of her throat with a razor.

[28] "Mouchette essaie de lutter contre ce silence…il l'enveloppe, elle a l'impression que la nappe invisible recouvre ses épaules, son front" (1329–30).

passages, in which Bernanos associates water with sounds, reinforce the importance of the "joyous sound" that Mouchette hears as she finally slides under the water. When the heroine gazes upon the quarry, the same silence in which she has already figuratively drowned returns. But as she slips under the water the silence is broken when Mouchette hears a "murmuring" that welcomes her (1345). Here Bernanos develops a direct relation between his heroine's drowning and the earlier passage in which he compared her *chant* to an inviting water: the situation has been reversed since the sound of the water now resembles a song. The final "joyous sound" that she hears announces her salvation.

The author emphasizes the purity and the calm of the clear water in which Mouchette drowns, accentuated by its transparence and implied source of snow from the mountains. These characteristics oppose the destructive rain and stagnant water found in the other parts of the novel. At the end of the narrative, the elements acquire a positive connotation, a sort of natural grace to accompany the divine grace that Bernanos seeks through God for his heroine. Furthermore, he repeats the adjective *douce* (gentle) three times and uses the adverb *doucement* (gently) in the final paragraphs: death's sweetness dominates the author's description of Mouchette's suicide. This *douceur* resembles the author's *style de la tendresse* and strongly contrasts with the violence of the storm, the rape, and the father's abuse inflicted on Mouchette from the beginning of the novel. All violence disappears at Mouchette's suicide.

The purity, gentleness, and clarity of the water evoke not only a peaceful rest but also the waters of baptism. In ascribing religious values to the novel, Michel Estève compares the *eau claire* in which Mouchette dies to "the spring water given to the Samaritan of the Gospels, which purifies and leads to eternal life."[29] Mouchette will emerge to a new life as suggested by the "the highest point in the sky" on which she fixes her gaze as she sinks into the water (1345). Her drowning then represents both death and rebirth: Mouchette achieves rebirth through her baptismal death. Water plays a central role in religious symbolism for Christians through its association with baptism and eternal life. In the rite of baptism, which is the first and most important sacrament, baptismal water is literally a substance of life: it purifies the soul by erasing sin, and bears the sign of the Christian's birth. Baptism itself, therefore, also contains both death and rebirth: the death to sin and the rising to new life, recalling Saint Paul's allusion to going down into death with Christ in baptism, so as to rise to new life with him.

---

[29] Michel Estève, *Bernanos: un triple itinéraire* (Paris: Hachette, 1981), p. 195.

Saving Mouchette

The author stresses the clarity of the (baptismal) water in which Mouchette drowns to distinguish it from the mud with which Mouchette has contact in the first three parts of the narrative. The absence of mud in the last part signifies the end of the heroine's inarticulate revolt against her misery and society. Among the numerous passages connecting Mouchette to mud, Bernanos makes three references to the heroine's deliberately covering her body with it, which proves to be an act of defiance (1281, 1316, and 1338). When she throws mud at her classmates, however, this provocation serves no purpose as the young girls continue to ignore Mouchette (1268). Other acts of defiance mark the heroine's contempt for society and her unconscious rebellion against misery: making noise with her clogs, refusing to interact or sing with her classmates, and declaring that Arsène is her lover. Nevertheless, these are only occasional acts of defiance since Mouchette usually rebels silently: her best defense against the villagers and the absence of love in her world is a rebellious silence. Seconds before her suicide, the heroine definitively gives up the fight.

With the end of her inarticulate revolt, Bernanos encourages his heroine to look to death in terms of rescue her from misery. Since Mouchette's life consists only of deprivation and suffering, Bernanos portrays her death as a *délivrance* and a way to purify her "stained life" (1339)—following the destruction of Mouchette's gift of song/self, she regains purity through death. The author even asserts that suicide has a different sense for the *misérables* because "their ignorance knows no escape except suicide—the suicide of the *misérable* resembles that of a child."[30] Thus for Bernanos the only escape for Mouchette, his *enfant misérable*, is suicide. Clearly he presents his heroine's suicide not as a defeat, but as an escape from the evil world in which a child's innocence can find no place. The reader notices that the way in which this Catholic novelist writes about his heroine's suicide removes the stigma of sin: the author-narrator's *douceur*, particularly in his description of the place and the manner in which she dies, exculpates her suicide. The heroine's idea of death is even associated with "tenderness" in the final scene (1339).

Bernanos proposes his heroine's salvation through her death. According to Michel Estève's formulation, this divine rescue occurs because the author-narrator "suggests the unsayable, the ineffable (*l'indicible*) of the sacred."[31] Mouchette's escape would then be offered by God because the author-narrator implies that her final encounter is with God, beyond the confines of

---

[30] "Il n'est sans doute d'autre ressource à leur ignorance que le suicide, le suicide du misérable, si pareil à celui de l'enfant" (1343).

[31] Michel Estève, *Bernanos: un triple itinéraire*, p. 198. Estève also argues that Mouchette's suicide affirms itself "as a quest for super-terrestrial value, for attaining another life," in *Le Sens de l'amour dans les romans de Bernanos* (Paris: Minard, 1959), p. 38.

the literary text. Bernanos seeks Mouchette's salvation *par un miracle de grâce* (1343), and makes her ultimate salvation clear in his *Vie de Jésus*: "The only way for the *misérables* to escape misery is through God."[32] The meaning of Mouchette's suicide is also suggested by the curé d'Ambricourt: "This misery…will awaken one day on the shoulder of Jesus."[33]

In truth, Mouchette's story resembles that of the curé, only stripped of its Christian context and language. Both novels contain the motifs of love—the curé's love for his parish and Mouchette's love for Arsène—as well as the suffering caused by the rejection of that love. The gift of self is an essential element of these motifs: Mouchette gives her purity/childhood to Arsène through her song and the curé offers himself to the countess. Agony is the price the curé and Mouchette must pay for the gift of self. While her acceptance of suffering is instinctive and non-Christian, the curé consciously accepts his suffering and that of others in *Imitatione Christi*. Agony, poverty, and childhood (examined in the life of the curé) represent the three conditions that are fused into the reality of Mouchette's short life. The curé's re-found childhood facilitates his acceptance of death as God's will, as he abandons himself to the "gentle mercy of God" (1230). Though Mouchette's purity/childhood is violated, Bernanos implies that she too will find it again in the gentle embrace of the *eau douce*.

Bernanos suggests that *tout est grâce* through Mouchette's death, though she certainly does not know it: the heroine becomes, in the curé's words, "one who has suffered in Christ" (1258). Along with his *style de la tendresse*, Bernanos assures his heroine's salvation through the symbolic passage from descent to ascension, from muddy to clear water, and from darkness to light. Although Mouchette moves from physical life to death, at the same time she emerges from spiritual death into spiritual life.

---

[32] Excerpts of this work are cited by Albert Béguin in *Bernanos par lui-même*, p. 188.

[33] "Une telle misère…doit se réveiller un jour sur l'épaule de Jésus-Christ" (1071).

CHAPTER 4
The Heroine's Salvation in Bresson's *Mouchette*

Although four films and sixteen years separate *Journal d'un curé de campagne* and *Mouchette*, Bresson's aesthetic conception remains essentially the same. The filmmaker's attitude concerning adaptation, however, changes significantly from one film to the other. While Bresson retains the first-person perspective of the novel to emphasize the curé's act of narrating in *Journal d'un curé de campagne*, he considerably alters the literary narration in *Mouchette* by eliminating the voice of the author-narrator and rejecting voice-over commentary.

The first-person narrative form of *Journal* allows the spectator access to interior "movements" and information, whereas in *Mouchette* all we know of the heroine is her behavior. The latter film is a visual study of the heroine's state of mind in that the filmmaker deliberately decides not to explain, or even hint at, her psychological motivations. Throughout *Mouchette* dramatic or emotional elements are found in Bresson's use of sounds (not in the minimal dialogue). The filmmaker then greatly diminishes the importance of language in *Mouchette*, as opposed to *Journal* in which the curé's voice-over often carries more weight than the images.

In transposing Bernanos' novel from the page to the screen, Bresson limits the spectator to an external perspective of the heroine, making no attempt to penetrate her consciousness. In Genette's terms, the narration of *Nouvelle Histoire de Mouchette* reveals "internal focalization" by focusing the narrative *through* the consciousness of the heroine, whereas Bresson employs "external focalization" in that his narrative focuses *on* the heroine.

The change in Bresson's attitude concerning adaptation is also evident in his own remarks, as he no longer seeks to "serve" Bernanos' text: "In *Journal d'un curé de campagne* I was more concerned with being faithful to the novel than being faithful to myself."[1] Bresson's inventions and additions in *Mouchette* illustrate this aspiration to *se servir* (and to *servir* his art of the *cinématographe*). In the first five of the film's eight sections, the majority of the scenes are the filmmaker's invention, that is, for the most part they are absent from the novel. In fewer instances, the "invented" scenes are based on minor or implicit incidents and descriptions found in the literary text so that the novelistic elements undergo various degrees of modification in the film. Bresson's additions include the weakening of the relationship between

---

[1] "Je me préoccupai de servir le livre [*Journal d'un curé de campagne*] au lieu de me servir." Robert Bresson, interview with Napoléon Murat in *Le Figaro littéraire*, March 16, 1967.

characters (Mouchette and Arsène), the emphasis on the relationship between characters (the Arsène-Mathieu-Louisa triangle), the increased visibility of characters (Louisa and the father), and finally, the displacement of literary passages.

Bresson stretches the narrative time of the novel as well. While Bernanos recounts less than the last twenty-four hours of Mouchette's life, the events of the film take place during more than one week since Bresson presents two Sundays; the day of the local fair (invented by the filmmaker) and that of the heroine's suicide. (Nevertheless, in both the novel and the film Mouchette loses her virginity and her mother the night before her suicide.) This broadening allows Bresson to introduce certain motifs in the opening sections in order to repeat them throughout the filmic narrative.

Furthermore, Bresson changes the location and the time period of the novel. He transposes the action from the Artois to the Vaucluse region, replacing the sinister atmosphere of the North with the less depressing environment of the South.[2] Bresson also modernizes the story, situating *Mouchette* in the 1960s instead of the 1930s, as is evident in the costumes, and the light rock/jazz music heard during the bumper car scene (clearly a Bressonian invention). According to Bresson's formulation, his film "suppresses the past," and in a sense, he also suppresses his heroine's personal history by transferring her recalled encounters to the present.[3] During the encounter with Arsène, for example, Bernanos fills his heroine's consciousness with images of her childhood. Among these memories, Mouchette recalls her father's smuggling (1278). On screen, Bresson shows the delivery of contraband alcohol by Mouchette's father and brother (section 3). While this change has its source in the literary text, it marks Bresson's transformative work in that the film remains rigorously in the present.

Setting Up the Film

The prologue section of the film begins with the image of a woman who is sitting, her face full of tears. We hear her mumble these words: "What will become of them without me?... This pain in my chest...as if I had a stone inside." From the very beginning, Bresson makes no effort to situate this person in a precise location and the semi-darkness contributes to the spectator's difficulty in identifying her. He opens the film with a medium shot, as opposed to an establishing shot that would permit the spectator to recognize the location as a church or to place the woman in the context of a village. The spectator learns these details only when the woman gets up and

---

[2] The filming of *Mouchette* took place in autumn (September through November of 1966), while Bernanos sets the story in "this desolate March" (1266).

[3] Robert Bresson, interview with Yvonne Baby in *Le Monde*, March 14, 1967.

leaves the image, thus creating an empty frame, which is a method that Bresson will use throughout his film. These first images of the film, due in part to the absence of establishing shots, introduce the spectator to ambiguity: s/he is disoriented, rather than comfortably entering the filmic space.

It is important to examine closely the words pronounced by the woman, whose identity is later revealed as Mouchette's mother. Her first sentence, a question (added by Bresson) that announces her death, seems to summarize Bernanos' description of the mother as the individual who "bears the whole weight of the family's misery" (1312).[4] The rest of her short monologue is only slightly reworked, but Bresson displaces these words pronounced by the mother from moments before her death (in the end of the second part of the novel) to the beginning of his film. In the literary text, the mother describes her agony to Mouchette: "The pain goes right up to my chest—it feels like a stone inside" (1308). When Bresson shows the mother's agony in the eighth section, he cuts out the majority of the mother-daughter conversation found in the novel.[5] The significant reduction of dialogue (throughout the film) is central to Bresson's emphasis on the soundtrack. The composition of natural sounds in *Mouchette* replaces the habitual dramatic function of dialogue in more conventional film (and in Bernanos' novel).

While looking at the empty frame, the spectator hears the clicking of the mother's footsteps on the stone floor of the church. The echo of her footsteps may be taken as a symbol of absence and futility: it reverberates in the empty shadows, evoking the isolation and helplessness of living in an indifferent and hostile world. Furthermore, the sound of the mother's footsteps effectively doubles the imminent menace suggested in her monologue. This sound fades as Monteverdi's *Magnificat* accompanies the credits that conclude the prologue section. The *Magnificat*—sacred music that symbolizes reconciliation and hope—is the only non-diegetic music (coming from "outside" the story) in the film, and will be heard once more at the moment of Mouchette's suicide, again with an empty frame. Bresson himself comments on the placement of this music at the beginning and the end: the film is then "enveloped by Christianity."[6] The music we hear functions as a

---

[4] The mother's question—"What will become of them without me?"—resembles a line found in the literary source of Bresson's *Une femme douce* (1969). At the end of Dostoevsky's "A Gentle Woman," the husband asks this question about his dead wife: "When they take her away tomorrow, what will become of me?" (A complete analysis of *Une femme douce* is found below in the conclusion.)

[5] Mouchette has only one lengthy encounter with her mother in the literary text (1298–1315), whereas in the film she has four shorter encounters with her mother (sections 3, 4, 6, and 8).

[6] Robert Bresson, interview with Yvonne Baby in *Le Monde*, March 14, 1967.

response to the mother's call (for help), as it will respond to her daughter's call at the end of the film.

The next section of the film prolongs certain motifs of the prologue and introduces other symbolic elements. Again the filmmaker shows his inclination toward fragmentation and the use of evocative sounds, but this time in a more developed manner. The first scene of this section, the longest and most important, is especially remarkable in presenting the sad destiny of trapped partridges. Filmed for the most part in close-ups, this scene reinforces the spectator's feeling of disorientation during the prologue section. The succession of images that focus on eyes, hands, objects (the snares), and birds (the partridges who unknowingly advance toward death), gives the spectator the impression that s/he is contemplating a disjointed and chaotic world, due to the under-contextualized nature of the images and the discontinuity of their organization. Most notably, with regard to the numerous images of pairs of eyes or of an individual eye, the spectator does not know to whom these eyes belong. Is it Mathieu who watches the poacher? Is it Arsène who spies on the prey? Bresson presumably wants to remove any point of reference so that the spectator remains unable to distinguish between the victim and the aggressor.

The abundant images of hands—also filmed in close-ups—produce a similar effect on the spectator who sees (the poacher's) hands setting traps, (the gamekeeper's) hands removing traps, and later (Madame Mathieu's) hands picking up traps. These hands often appear to be autonomous appendages, as Bresson explained: "Hands often have a 'life' independent of their owner."[7] Since the hands on screen seem detached from the body, they can create the impression for the spectator that what is happening before him/her occurs inevitably.[8]

The partridge scene, marked by the complete absence of conversation, is followed by four scenes that contain only two short lines. In the fourth scene of the second section, Bresson presents Mathieu walking home and we hear one word, the heroine's name. Here the viewer sees Mouchette for the first time: she watches the gamekeeper pass by the school as a classmate calls out to the distracted heroine, "Mouchette!"[9] (Apart from singing and humming, the heroine does not speak until her encounter with Arsène in the seventh section.) Upon returning home, Mathieu throws the traps on the kitchen table

---

[7] Pierre Ajame, "Le Cinéma selon Bresson," *Les Nouvelles littéraires* 26 (May 1966), p. 14.

[8] In the novel, when Mouchette looks at her hands just before her suicide, her *main brune* seems detached from her body (1340).

[9] When the novel begins, the heroine has already left school (and observes her teacher and classmates from a hilltop). In the film she goes to school three times.

and murmurs to his wife: "Him again!" As elsewhere, Bresson replaces dialogue with evocative sounds in this section.

The filmmaker amplifies background noises to prolong the tone established in the first scene of the film. These are dry sounds: the rustling of leaves, the cracking and breaking of branches, the panicked beating of wings (as a partridge desperately struggles in vain), and the heavy step of Mathieu's steel-tipped shoes on the road. The effect of these sounds, which emphasize the violence of the images, suggests that the viewer encounters much more than a simple poaching. Furthermore, Bresson uses contrasting tones as an aural counterpoint to evoke the image of another world, beyond the one before the spectator's eyes, in which life is calm and perhaps happy: in the beginning of the section we hear dogs barking in the distance, and at the end, we hear the chatter and laughter of children.

The main function of the second section is a symbolic one: the vulnerable partridge, an innocent victim who struggles in vain, may be taken as representing Mouchette. The young girl will endure the same pitiless fate, and will fall victim to sudden and undeserved violence. The cruel irony here is that in both cases the aggressor is the same: Arsène lays the traps and violates the heroine. Yet Bresson also presents the image of a partridge freed by Mathieu; the camera follows the bird (in a rare panning shot) as it flies up to the sky. Bresson emphasizes this image by inserting it again, preceded by the same loud flapping of wings, in the sixth section. This time Bresson directly associates Mouchette with the bird, given that the heroine watches the second liberating flight. These images of liberation relate to the heroine's death, as Bresson told Georges Sadoul: "For Bernanos, and for me, Mouchette's suicide is not an end, but a beginning."[10]

Bresson establishes the motifs of his film in the opening sections. During the partridge scene, the spectator may struggle to interpret the images of cruelty and violence, which represent an underlying motif of the film. This violence and the analogy between the birds' destiny and that of Mouchette become more explicit in the penultimate scene of the film (also absent from the literary text) in which Mouchette heads toward the pond where she will kill herself. In what appears to be a cinematic response or homage to Jean Renoir's *La Règle du jeu* (1939), Bresson shows us a massacre of hares by hunters. It is also possible that he expands on the following literary description: Arsène's bag, which falls to the floor, "was full of hares, not yet stiff, sticky and glistening with blood" (1274).

Throughout the novel, Bernanos describes his heroine as a "hunted animal" to illustrate her situation, frequently likening her to animals, such as

---

[10] Georges Sadoul, "Conversation plutôt qu'interview avec Robert Bresson sur *Mouchette*," *Les Lettres françaises* 1174 (March 1967), p. 18.

hares, *partridges*, and cats. On screen, Bresson shows her as a *bête traquée* during the singing lesson when Madame grabs and holds her neck, recalling the noose that strangles the partridge (section 4), and in the *buvette* when she jumps out from under the table (to escape Arsène) as would a hare (section 7).[11] Bresson also shows Mouchette curled up in the foliage after the rape, creating a visual transposition of the literary passage in which she "occupies hardly more space than a hare" (1296). Finally, Bresson presents a counter-shot of Mouchette after Mathieu's wife pronounces the word "hare" in the last section of the film, which has the effect of associating the heroine with game.

Bresson's familiarity with the Rousseaux interview (in which Bernanos compares Mouchette's death to that of a defeated bull) may explain why the filmmaker "intuitively" introduces animals whose sad destiny symbolizes the heroine's fate.[12] A second source in provoking the filmmaker's "intuition" is *Au hasard Balthazar*, the film that Bresson completed just months before filming *Mouchette*.[13] Both films depict the limits of suffering and humiliation that a living being (human and animal) can bear. The affinity between these two films is striking: even for the viewer who knows Bernanos' text, the two films, as much as the novel and the film, seem to echo each other, each as a sort of continuation of the other. In both films there is a doubling of the human and animal: in *Au hasard Balthazar* Marie's story is parallel to that of the donkey, whose suffering prefigures her own, just as the slaughter of the hares and the strangling of the partridges prefigure Mouchette's destiny. For Bresson, both Mouchette and the donkey are "prey to public cruelty."[14] (It is interesting to note that in both films the same *modèle*, Jean-Claude Guilbert, incarnates two different characters, Arnold in *Au hasard Balthazar* and Arsène in *Mouchette*, which is exceptional in Bresson's *œuvre*. Both characters are drunk *révoltés* living apart from society, which furthers the idea of continuity between the two films.)

The two scenes in *Mouchette* depicting the hunt evoke what Bernanos called (in the Rosseaux interview) the *malheur et injustice* imposed on his heroine.[15] Yet the hare scene not only anticipates Mouchette's death, its brutality strikes the spectator. Bresson connects Mouchette with the violence

---

[11] In the novel, the rape takes place in a *cabane* (hut) called *le Rendez-Vous* (1282). Bresson refers to this *cabane* as a *buvette* (refreshment stand) in the script.

[12] Georges Sadoul, "Conversation plutôt qu'interview," p. 18.

[13] Making two films in two years marks a change in Bresson's output. In discussing *Mouchette* with Yvonne Baby, the filmmaker explained that he accepted the request made by the Bernanos family because time constraints forced him to "adapt more than invent," in *Le Monde*, March 14, 1967.

[14] Ibid.

[15] Michel Estève, *Bernanos* (Paris: Gallimard, 1965), p. 243.

and death of the hare massacre because she is a witness to it. The filmmaker abandons the elliptical style he used when filming the partridges to momentarily adopt the heroine's point of view by alternating (in shot-reverse shot) images of the hunters, the hares, and Mouchette's reactions: she is panic-stricken and ends up running away.

In this scene the viewer watches the conclusion of a movement that began with the symbolism of the first sections. Again the soundtrack plays a crucial role: before the heroine sees the dying animals, the spectator hears the barking of hunting dogs and detonations that recall the cracking and breaking of branches in the partridge scene, as well as the footsteps that resonated in the silence of the church in the prologue. Through the vicious massacre of hares, Bresson accomplishes what the first symbolic scene suggested: the spectator encounters a hostile world in which innocent, defenseless beings are prey to an arbitrary evil. This is Mouchette's world. The symbolism of the two hunting scenes, which are absent from the novel, then suggests that for Bresson the suicide is the result of a general condition.

The Refusal of Psychology

Bresson not only inserts new elements in his film, he also alters existing elements of the novel in accordance with the components of his medium and his *œuvre*. Even when Bresson retains the main point of a literary passage, the cinematic result typically differs from the literary text. The singing lesson provides an excellent example.[16] In both the novel and the film, this scene holds the same function: it serves as an introduction to the heroine's character (even though Bresson transfers what occurs on the first pages of the novel to the beginning of the fourth section of his film). A comparison of this scene in the literary and filmic texts reveals the different aesthetic strategies that each author employs to show the subsequent evolution of the heroine's character.

The first important difference between the two presentations of this scene concerns the distinction between present and past—the event takes place in the present on screen, while Bernanos explains Mouchette's recollection of the singing lesson in which she was a reluctant participant. Secondly, we encounter the strong opposition between an event viewed externally (on screen) and the interiorization of an experience (in the novel). Consequently, the literary version is more psychologically complex. The reader senses the intensity of Mouchette's feelings resulting from confrontations with Madame—her memories appear to be a merging of several excruciating

---

[16] The lyrics of the song (sung by Mouchette and her classmates on screen and in the novel) are the words of encouragement that Columbus addressed to his sailors just before discovering the continent in 1492.

lessons—and from the extended duration of her "cruel struggle" (1267).[17] Mouchette obstinately refuses to reveal her beautiful voice—her purity—in spite of the teacher's threats and the humiliation she will endure from her classmates. Bresson, on the other hand, removes all references to Mouchette's *voix charmante*: the spectator hears only "a raucous voice and wrong notes" (according to Bresson's script) so that the scene lacks the information provided by Bernanos about his heroine's inner state.[18]

In the novel, the "painful nature" of each note causes Mouchette to cry, marking her reluctance to reveal the innermost part of herself (1266). Her tears prefigure the author-narrator's correlation between his heroine's voice and her purity/virginity in the form of "tears of shame" (1305). The heroine's shame will then be associated with the purity of her song. The singing lesson announces the purity motif (which will be further developed by the author-narrator) by revealing that the heroine's *chant* represents her gift of self. Bresson removes this psychological orientation of the scene.

On screen, the singing lesson scene seems to have been conceived according to the motifs already presented through images and sounds in the opening sections. This time it is Madame who spies on and grabs her vulnerable prey. The viewer again hears noises that are transformed into evocative sounds: heavy footsteps that resonated in the church and on the road become the scraping noise of Mouchette's oversized and worn-out clogs (a sound that breaks the silence in the classroom, as she is the last pupil to arrive). The heroine drags her feet not just to infuriate Madame but also to show her revolt. Her refusal to sing, on the other hand, is a silent act of defiance (as in the novel).

Bresson shows the futility of Mouchette's defiance by emphasizing Madame's violent gestures. The teacher compels the heroine to sing by shoving her in the back, seizing her by the neck, and forcing her to bend over the piano. Through these images, Bresson expands on the literary passage, which contains only one instance of Madame's cruel actions. At the end of the lesson in the film, Mouchette hides her face in her hands, a sign of being defeated by her teacher. This gesture also indicates that she will have to cede to hostile forces that surpass her capacity of defense.

In the novel, through the singing lesson, the reader encounters the author's psychological presentation of his heroine, from which other motifs, such as purity, are elaborated.[19] In the film, the spectator encounters a

---

[17] Bresson uses dissolves at the beginning and end of the singing lesson to suggest the duration of what Bernanos calls the *lutte inégale* whose "cruelty no one would ever know" (1267).

[18] Robert Bresson, *"Mouchette*: découpage," *L'Avant-scène* 80 (1968), p. 10.

[19] Given that Bresson significantly abridges Mouchette's encounter with the *visiteuse des morts*, he eliminates the important (literary) correlation between the idea of death and the image of purity. He also neutralizes the character by calling her the *visiteuse* (visitor) in the script, rather

presentation of the heroine without psychological notations, which Bresson links to already established motifs, thus connecting the scene to the general symbolism of the film. The singing lesson illustrates the filmmaker's refusal to reveal the heroine's emotional motivations: "If there is analysis and psychology in my films, it is with images and in the manner of portrait-painters."[20] Since Bresson purges his work of psychological inclinations, the spectator does not have access to Mouchette's consciousness as provided by the author-narrator's commentary throughout the novel.

The refusal of psychological motivation is also evident in Bresson's reworking and displacement of the cyclone motif. When Bernanos begins his novel by adopting his heroine's point of view to describe the arrival of the storm, the reader shares her instinctive perceptions of the wind that (for her) will be transformed into a cyclone. The storm is present in the film, but Bresson transfers it to the end of the sixth section. (This displacement then precludes Bresson from showing the evolution of darkness to light, of night to day: while the film begins with the dark interior of the church, the clarity of several outdoor scenes precedes the nocturnal storm.) The storm remains one of the actions that the spectator hears and views externally, while in the novel the cyclone ravages Mouchette's fragile consciousness. Clearly Bresson makes a great effort to respect the aural and acoustic nature of the storm, but the spectator's experience differs greatly from that of the reader, for whom the psychological implications of the cyclone reveal the heroine's dream-like experience.

In the novel, Mouchette loses her purity for an illusion in perceiving an ordinary windstorm as a cyclone, which explains to the reader why she is "duped by a dream, not a man" (1311). In transforming the real events of her encounter with the poacher into a dream—the cyclone blows only in her imagination—she dies a victim of her dreams. In Bresson's film, she dies a victim of a violent and cruel society. The filmmaker significantly abridges the heroine's conversation with the poacher to remove the tale of the cyclone Arsène had witnessed as a boy, which captivates Mouchette and deepens her belief in the reality of the present "cyclone." This suppression of Arsène's tale not only reflects Bresson's principle of remaining in the present, it also limits the viewer to an external perspective: the storm loses its privileged initial position of the novel and no longer becomes the substance of the heroine's dreams. The filmmaker's purging of the novel's psychological elements explains the removal of these dream-like dimensions. As a result of what he called his "distrust of analysis and psychology," Bresson denies the

---

than the *veilleuse* (protector) as in the novel.

[20] Robert Bresson, interview with Yvonne Baby in *Le Monde*, March 14, 1967.

spectator access to the heroine's consciousness throughout the filmic narrative.[21]

Characters and Their Relations

The viewer has extremely limited access to Mouchette's perceptions of and feelings for the poacher, which are omnipresent in the novel through the author-narrator's position "inside" his heroine's consciousness. Bresson rejects two important literary passages in which Arsène admires Mouchette, the second of which contains his last lines to her before the rape (1283 and 1295). By omitting these passages, the filmmaker suppresses rare words of kindness for Mouchette—words that connect her to the poacher.

Before Arsène's fit, Bernanos interrupts the dialogue to reveal his heroine's inner feelings as she looks at Arsène's face, suggesting her awakening of love (1289). Bresson omits this passage, but retains the lines of dialogue from the literary text that precede and follow it. Furthermore, since Mouchette does not look at Arsène during this part of the scene, Bresson refuses to show her *plaisir* in contemplating his face (1288). On screen, the heroine's attraction to him comes only from their shared resentment for the village. In the novel, Mouchette feels affection for Arsène (and even trusts him enough to take his hand, a gesture that is absent on screen), and therefore is raped by the man she "loves." The emotional connection between the two members of the tragic couple is missing in the film: the spectator is unaware of her feelings for the poacher because s/he does not have access to the heroine's interior monologue.

While Bernanos further develops this connection through the cyclone motif, Bresson alters the presentation of Arsène's account of his fight with Mathieu. In the novel, this account contains important references to the "cyclone" and reveals Arsène's confidence in the heroine. On screen, the spectator witnesses the violent fight between the poacher and the gamekeeper, encountering the same elements and characters presented in the partridge scene. The action again takes place in the woods where the poacher repeats the gesture of laying out traps, although this time Arsène himself becomes the prey because Mathieu catches him. Murderous hands reappear in this scene: Bresson gives a close-up of Arsène's hand attempting to strangle Mathieu, which the gamekeeper then bites.

In dramatizing Arsène's oral account, framed by two shots of the moon and moving clouds, Bresson weakens the Mouchette-Arsène relationship. In the novel, Arsène describes to Mouchette a *sacré cyclone* during his fight with Mathieu (1286). She believes his story, and transforms the present windstorm into a cyclone in her mind: this dream further connects her to the

---

[21] Ibid.

companion whom she admires and who in turn admires her. In the novel, then, by recounting his fight with Mathieu to Mouchette, Arsène offers her a feeling of mutual complicity and an acceptance she has never known.

During the fight scene, the camera never leaves Arsène and Mathieu: Bresson turns his camera toward Mouchette only after the scuffle. The filmmaker therefore refuses to directly link the heroine to the brutality of the brawl, in spite of the fact that she is the victim of so many forms of violence throughout the film. Yet Mouchette sees the confrontation with her own eyes (becoming a spectator) so that her attitude toward the poacher and the fantastic story he recounts is greatly modified from that of the novel: she is less connected to her aggressor, no longer being the intended recipient of a narrative, but an unseen witness of a violent confrontation. The filmmaker's suppression of the author-narrator's commentary and his reduction of the literary dialogue concerning the cyclone deprive the film of the dream-like dimensions found in the novel, which are particularly important in connecting the heroine to the man who rapes her.

In addition to rejecting the emotional connection between Mouchette and her aggressor, Bresson also augments the violence that precedes the rape.[22] First, he presents gestures and sounds that recall the preceding images of violence in the film. In the beginning of the rape scene (section 7), Arsène kneels to light a fire, just as he knelt to set the traps in the partridge scene. Certain sounds, too, are reminiscent of those heard in the opening sections: we hear the scraping sound of Mouchette's clogs, but this symbol of her revolt is covered by other sounds, in particular the crackling of the fire as the flames noisily consume the branches, recalling the sound of cracking branches. Secondly, Bresson shows the entire epileptic fit (rather than employing ellipsis), perhaps to emphasize the importance of the heroine's song, which momentarily immobilizes the rhythm of the film. During Arsène's fit, Mouchette is finally able to sing in tune: she cradles the poacher's head and wipes slaver from his face, as in the novel, but her action of singing loses some of its extraordinary quality when rendered by the camera and microphone.[23] In the novel, Bernanos clearly associates Mouchette's gift of song with the gift of her body: her *chant* is the symbol of her purity. Bresson's *modèle*, Nadine Nortier, may have a beautiful voice, but her song does not equal the fragile purity suggested by Bernanos' words:

---

[22] Arsène sees Mouchette for the first time on screen right after his *violent* confrontation with Mathieu in the opening scenes of section 7 and rapes her at the end of that section.

[23] On screen, Mouchette sings the Columbus song about *hope* before the rape (and then at home, where her mother is dying). In the novel, Mouchette sings "a Negro dance-tune, as they called it [which she would hum softly to fall asleep again after being awakened by her drunken father's return]. She had never been able to get it out of her head, unlike Madame's tunes, which she could never keep there" (1291).

"Mouchette's song refreshes her body and her soul like a pure liquid in which she would like to immerse her hands" (1292). Once again Bresson denies the viewer access to the interiority of the character.

Thirdly, the heroine's struggle and resistance render the rape scene more violent on screen than in the novel. Since Bresson chooses to not establish emotional ties between the two characters, Mouchette fights furiously, like the partridges, in an effort to liberate herself. As Arsène tries to seize his prey, Mouchette escapes momentarily. During the chase, the aggressor breaks glasses that explode like firecrackers, and violently kicks over the table and chairs under which Mouchette hides like a frightened animal. The table then tumbles down noisily on the cement. (More intense and explicit, these noises nevertheless have the same character as the mother's footsteps on the stone in the church.) Mouchette resists, but, as implied by this uproar of threatening sounds, there is no way out. The spectator sees a close-up of her legs retreating; the girl trips on a bundle of sticks and falls backward. Arsène then throws himself on her. Instead of hearing Arsène's *souffle* (as in the literary text), the spectator hears only the continuous crackling of the fire, possibly suggesting the fires of hell.

Bresson's images of the rape extend beyond the description found in the literary text, as will be the case with the suicide scene. On screen, the heroine performs gestures that are invented by Bresson: she flails her arms in a vain attempt to resist Arsène, but finally submits and accepts what is imposed on her. The fact that the heroine *embraces her aggressor* is a sad reminder of her potential for tenderness.[24] (Likewise, Bresson stresses this potential in every scene with Mouchette and her mother: the heroine shows her emotion through gestures, such as kissing her mother's hand, which does not occur in the novel.) Bresson gives the spectator a glimpse of what her life *could* be, in spite of its being a loveless existence.

Early in the film, Bresson introduces a conflict that greatly impacts the rape. Bernanos refers to this conflict only once in the novel, when Arsène recounts to Mouchette what Mathieu had told him during their fight: "I'm warning you to leave Louisa alone—I don't like people messing with me, especially when it comes to women" (1286).[25] Bernanos fails to give further explanation to this remark. On screen, however, Louisa is an important character who appears in seven scenes. During the fight scene in the film, the spectator already knows about Arsène and Mathieu's rivalry concerning

---

[24] In Catherine Breillat's *À ma sœur* (2001), the young heroine, Anaïs, embraces her rapist in the pivotal penultimate scene of the film—perhaps in cinematic homage to Bresson.

[25] Contrary to the analysis of certain critics (such as Georges Charensol and Jean Sémolué), Bresson does not "invent" the Louisa character.

Louisa, yet Bresson stresses the importance of her role by having the two rivals repeat her name three times before their brawl erupts (section 7).

Louisa's role inflates the professional animosity between Arsène and Mathieu in that Bresson explicitly presents her as the reason for the sexual rivalry between the poacher and the gamekeeper: we see her encourage Arsène and turn down Mathieu's advances (section 3).[26] Louisa first appears behind the bar at the café while serving Arsène a drink and drying a glass. When he leaves, the barmaid washes and dries his glass, and with Mathieu's entrance into the café, she again pours a drink. The minimal dialogue, invented by Bresson, reveals that Louisa encourages Arsène by asking him to return. As for the gamekeeper, Louisa quickly disengages his hand with a look of disapproval. These encounters between Arsène and Louisa, and then Mathieu and Louisa, allow the viewer to assume that this competition has continued on for some time.[27]

Bresson begins the fifth section of his film with a medium shot of hands washing glasses behind the bar. The viewer thinks it is Louisa washing the glasses, but the camera dollies back to reveal it is Mouchette. The spectator sees Mouchette behind the same bar performing the same actions as Louisa, rinsing and drying glasses. With this important shot Bresson identifies Mouchette with Louisa.

The filmmaker establishes a clear parallel between these two characters (and it appears that Louisa somewhat threatens Mouchette's status as the central female character). In the fourth section, Louisa avoids Mathieu's eager grasp as he pursues her in the poorly lit cellar of the café.[28] This scene prefigures the rape of Mouchette, and in particular parallels Arsène's pursuit of Mouchette in the gloomy, somber interior of the *buvette* (section 7). This parallelism between the two then acquires more significance once the filmmaker has associated Mouchette with Louisa (behind the bar).

During the *fête villageoise*, the filmmaker juxtaposes scenes with Mouchette and Louisa (section 5). Images of Mouchette and an adolescent boy on the bumper cars are followed by those of Arsène and Louisa on an airplane ride, extending the parallelism between the heroine and the barmaid.

---

[26] In Renoir's *La Règle du jeu*, the professional rivalry between the gamekeeper and the poacher becomes a private conflict when the latter pursues the former's wife. The spectator encounters a similar triangular relationship in *Mouchette*.

[27] Bresson also invents a dialogue in which a villager taunts Mathieu about Arsène to suggest that everyone knows about the rivalry concerning Louisa. (Her name recalls the governess in *Journal d'un curé de campagne*.)

[28] Here Bresson invents their dialogue (as with every conversation involving Louisa) in which Mathieu accuses Louisa of "loving another man." Later in the film (after the *fête villageoise*), Mathieu tells her that Arsène must be in love with her, to which she replies : "You're too scared of him to do anything about it" (section 5).

The spectator hears the repeated sound of an anonymous whistle, which announces the "take off" of the tiny planes. But there is no real departure: as with the bumper cars, these planes embark on a circular journey that leads nowhere. We then discover that both female characters are being watched: Mathieu stalks Louisa, and Mouchette's father spies on his daughter.

Bresson's own remarks hint at why he stresses Louisa's role in the film. He said that his greatest challenge was "to make *Mouchette* bearable without softening it."[29] He accomplishes this by presenting a character who appears in situations that are parallel to those of the heroine. The parallelism is a then way of commenting on the lamentable condition that Mouchette endures. The greatly increased importance of Louisa's role in the film supports Bresson's belief that life is made up of "predestination and chance (*hasard*)."[30] Due to Louisa's presence, the rape has more of an accidental character—Bresson shows Arsène with a girlfriend. Since Louisa has a more significant rapport with the poacher than does Mouchette, the heroine is victim of the whims of *hasard* and the rape becomes readable as an act of chance.[31]

Sounds, Symbols, and Sensibilities

As with Louisa's role, Bresson also increases the visibility of Mouchette's father. In the novel, the father is clearly a secondary character: though he figures in the heroine's recollections, he is only physically present the morning following his wife's death. On screen, the father plays a much more significant role. Bresson adds scenes that feature this brutal and drunk character to amplify the violence motif through sounds associated with the father's abuse.

In the third section of *Mouchette*, when the father delivers cases of alcohol to the café, the viewer hears the slamming of his truck door. Bresson repeats this metallic sound (which echoes the suggestive sounds of the first two sections) two more times, and the last time the slamming sound is particularly violent. This sound connects with the final section of the film, which begins with the dreadful (off-screen) slamming of the door of the house in which the mother has just died: this slam marks the return of the father and son. Bresson presents a man who closes doors and shoves his daughter with the same brute force. The father's behavior reflects an arbitrary, unjust, and irrational violence of which Mouchette is the victim throughout the film.

---

[29] Robert Bresson, interview with Napoléon Murat in *Le Figaro littéraire*, March 16, 1967.

[30] Robert Bresson, interview with Jean-Luc Godard and Michel Delahaye in *Cahiers du cinéma* 178 (May 1966), p. 30.

[31] When Arsène encounters Mouchette for the first time on screen, Bresson alters the literary dialogue to imply more of a chance meeting than in the novel.

During the delivery, the spectator hears another striking noise that will become one of the recurring sounds in the rest of the film—the sound of trucks that pass by on the road. At the beginning of the scene, we hear the humming of the motor of the father's truck, followed by the sound of the motor of a police car, which appears in front of the café. Next, we see the father's vehicle returning home as it zigzags from one side of the road to the other (he is obviously drunk), almost crashing into other trucks that pass loudly in the opposite direction. Bresson then cuts to the interior of the house where Mouchette tends to her dying mother and bawling baby brother. The heroine hears the sound of her father's truck and sees the flash of its headlights. The father and brother enter the house, and without speaking or looking at his wife, the father flops down onto a straw mattress: using his cap as an imaginary steering wheel, he begins to imitate the sound of a motor. This *monologue bruité*, as Bresson calls it in the script, continues off-screen throughout this scene.[32]

The use of sound in this section illustrates Bresson's assertion that sound in his film "suggests what Bernanos wrote."[33] The motor sound is heard at crucial moments throughout the rest of the film to amplify the motif of unmotivated violence and rage suggested by the person with whom it is initially associated, the father. Beyond this, the sound becomes a symbolic element that represents the general condition that crushes Mouchette: when she waits for the poacher outside the closed café, for example, trucks reappear (with the racket and flash of headlights that accompany their passing) to foreshadow Arsène's violence (section 7).

Mouchette's arrival at home after the rape is also accompanied by the sound of a truck motor. Trucks continue to roll along through the night, but their humming noise becomes roaring when the mother's death rattle begins, as if to announce her death. Then the baby's wailing and the passing of another truck respond as if to cruelly muffle the mother's agony. The viewer hears the noise of passing trucks three times in this scene, which in part prevents Mouchette from confessing to her mother. (The fact that it often occurs off-screen, or is heard during the night, makes it more threatening.)

On the morning of her own death, as Mouchette heads for Mathieu's house, the spectator again hears the sound of motors (section 8). The violent character of this noise has diminished, however, as the sound now comes from car, not truck, motors. This time the ringing of church bells replaces the baby's cries to mix with the sound.[34] In the moments preceding Mouchette's

---

[32] Robert Bresson, "*Mouchette*: découpage," p. 12.

[33] Georges Sadoul, "Conversation plutôt qu'interview," p. 18.

[34] Church bells ring four times on the first Sunday morning in the film, and eight times on the second Sunday (sections 4 and 8).

death, the viewer once again hears the sound of a motor: a tractor replaces the horse belonging to Ménétrier, the farmer in the novel.[35] This substitution allows Bresson to connect this sound motif, whose origin goes back to the beginning of the film, with the heroine's suicide. Mouchette attempts to shout out a few words to the old man, but he continues on his way; her voice drowns in the tractor's whirring, just as she will drown in the water.

Like the images of the strangled partridges and the dead hares, also accompanied by important sounds, the rumble of the motors is essentially a symbolic (even emotional) element. Through this expressive sound, Bresson suggests that what pushes Mouchette to suicide is not just Arsène's violence: the filmic universe is impregnated with a malicious force represented by a mechanical sound. The soundtrack is clearly one of the most significant components of the film. Bresson uses sounds to replace dialogue, and their opposition to the general muteness of the film renders them even more intense. While Bernanos evokes Mouchette's experience through auditory terms and constant references to sound, allowing the reader to enter her world of senses and instinct, Bresson communicates the condition that crushes Mouchette through his use of sound(s).

The filmmaker also conveys that condition by means of looks or gestures in that characters often "speak" using glances, not words. Bresson introduces the *regard* motif in the partridge scene through close-ups of eyes that translate a potentially violent relationship with the object of their gaze.[36] Certainly the gaze and death are linked in that scene, but violence in the gaze takes on other forms as well. In the last section of the film, for example, the grocer and her client, as well as three women entering the church, look upon Mouchette with disdain. These looks represent the progressive abuse that the heroine suffers at the hands of the villagers. Bresson also shows this indifference, or what he calls "voluntary blindness," (represented by the tractor driver) to expose the cruel condition that defeats the heroine.[37]

In addition to using sounds and glances, Bresson communicates Mouchette's defeat by society through the repetition of images, which provides an important structural component of his film. The filmmaker establishes the use of repetition in the opening sections with recurring shots of hands, eyes, traps, and struggling partridges, in order to suggest the violence and cruelty in Mouchette's world. Bresson then repeats images of cruelty (by the father, the teacher, and Arsène) throughout the film. Twice the father enters the frame to shove his daughter, and Arsène's action of seizing Mathieu's neck

---

[35] In the literary text, Mouchette hears the hoofs of the horse before seeing Ménétrier (1344).

[36] The spectator encounters this motif in the rest of the film through the repetition of images in which characters look out the window.

[37] Georges Sadoul, "Conversation plutôt qu'interview," p. 18.

echoes Madame's action of grabbing Mouchette's neck in the singing lesson scene. (Mouchette endures cruelty from children as well: two boys mock her with obscene gestures and call her names in sections 4 and 8).

Through repetition, Bresson also emphasizes images related to mud—a symbol of the heroine's rebellion against her detested society in both the film and the novel. We see Mouchette stamp her feet in a mud puddle in front of the church (section 4), and throw mud two times at her classmates (sections 4 and 6).[38] The latter gesture marks the only communication between Mouchette and the other students. Bresson further emphasizes the heroine's revolt through repeated images and sounds that are associated with her clogs. We hear the clunking sound of Mouchette's clogs throughout the film (ten times); it is an aural sign of her revolt that often continues over a cut to the next shot. In order to emphasize this symbol of her revolt, Bresson films Mouchette's legs as she enters the classroom or walks on the road. In the last section both signs of her revolt are combined when Mouchette rubs mud (twice) into the rug with her clogs. This gesture is not found in the novel; Bresson adds the heroine's final on-screen sign of revolt.

The most repeated image in the film is that of hands, first shown in the partridge scene. By repeating images of (autonomous) hands, Bresson forces the spectator to work at determining to whom hands belong and, more importantly, whether the hands have kind or cruel intentions. The hands of the teacher, the father, and Arsène have cruel intentions. In the cellar of the café, the hands that freed the partridges (Mathieu's hands) become those of the aggressor, as the gamekeeper pursues Louisa. In the novel, Bernanos locates the physical nature of Mouchette's inheritance of misery in her hands, but on screen hands are less a sign of misery than a symbol of the cruel, loveless condition that defeats her.

The Kindness of Strangers

Hands are not always cruel in Bresson's film. There is one instance in which hands give symbolic comfort to Mouchette, standing out in contrast to the repeated images of unkind hands. During the *fête villageoise* in the fifth section, Bresson presents a shot in which an anonymous female buys a token. The next shot reveals a young woman with a baby in her arms, who passed behind Mouchette in the crowd moments earlier. Bresson then shows this woman's hand placing the token into Mouchette's, and another shot reveals the heroine's surprise as the stranger exits the frame. (Here we encounter a

---

[38] These gestures are found in the novel. While Bresson shows many of the heroine's physical actions of the literary text, he suppresses the mental processes and the interior monologues that accompany and explain them. Mouchette also performs actions (with dexterity) that are added by Bresson, such as preparing coffee and refilling a gin bottle with water (sections 4 and 8). In the novel, Mouchette recalls her mother's action of refilling a gin bottle (1271).

mother who gives to Mouchette what her own mother fails to provide.) At first, the spectator does not know to whom this hand belongs, and Mouchette receives the gift without speaking to the young woman.

This mysterious woman represents the cinematic transposition of the tall fair-haired girl who caressed the heroine's cheek in the novel (1341). Just before Mouchette's suicide, the author-narrator describes this memory of the single act of tenderness in her life (though the encounter marks the beginning of the heroine's rebellion against tenderness). This *rencontre*, containing literary images of kind hands, took place during a *fête*. As with many of Bresson's additions, the token scene corresponds to an event suggested by the author of the literary text.

Upon receiving the token, the heroine uses it to take a ride on the bumper cars. As Mouchette sits behind the wheel, she undergoes a complete metamorphosis: in contrast with her usually withdrawn character, here Mouchette blooms into a joyous girl whose face radiates with a smile and even laughter. During this scene, the spectator witnesses her transcendent moment of elation. For an instant, the heroine's sense of freedom (from violence) prefigures her liberation at the end of the film. While Bernanos' heroine temporarily transcends her destitute condition through her song, creating one moment of joy in her life of misery, on screen this moment of joy occurs on a bumper car ride (invented by Bresson).[39] We finally see the heroine as a playful girl. Throughout the film the child encounters hostile forces that suffocate her, with the exception of this one episode of happiness.

This scene includes another important innovation by Bresson in relation to the novel. The filmmaker presents an innocent flirtation and exchange of smiles between the heroine and someone close to her age: an adolescent boy (in another bumper car) playfully hits her car and smiles, as an innocent game of tag ensues.[40] Bresson commented on his goal in inventing the local fair and the boy to whom Mouchette is attracted: "The vanishing of hope does not necessarily lead to despair...happiness makes the darkness (*le noir*), the somberness of what follows stand out better."[41] The spectator is struck by the stark contrast between the image of a radiant Mouchette and the *noir* of her later encounters (the rape, her mother's death, and the villagers' cruelty).

After the ride is over, Mouchette follows the boy who gently turns around to look at his timid companion. However, before they can exchange a word, hands seize Mouchette's shoulders: her father violently shoves and

[39] In Jean-Pierre and Luc Dardenne's *La Promesse* (1996), the young hero, Igor, experiences a similar moment of joy riding on a go-cart, which marks one of many examples of Bressonian influence in the films of the Dardenne brothers.

[40] In spite of the mock violence (seen in the crashing of bumper cars) and the fact that the heroine is once again pursued, here the ritual chase is a happy and liberating one.

[41] Robert Bresson, interview with Napoléon Murat in *Le Figaro littéraire*, March 16, 1967.

slaps his daughter. Ironically, the mysterious woman's act of kindness brings about the father's violence: caring hands are replaced by brutal ones that inflict an arbitrary and unjust punishment upon the heroine.[42] Therefore the instrument that facilitates the heroine's burst of happiness also reinforces Bresson's suggestion of the cruel condition in which Mouchette is condemned to live. Just as her affection for her mother suggests that she could have a love-filled existence, Mouchette's smiles in the bumper car scene show her potential for tenderness and for having a normal life with other children her age, instead of a tragic destiny.

Death and Subjectivity

Bresson's refusal to provide the spectator access to the interiority of the heroine is particularly apparent in his treatment of Mouchette's suicide. While Bresson does not hint at any forethought concerning her death, Bernanos enters his heroine's consciousness to explain her innermost thoughts in the final pages of the novel: "Now she was thinking of her own death, with her heart gripped not by fear but by the excitement of a great discovery, the feeling that she was about to learn what she had been unable to learn from her brief experience of love" (1339). On the last page of the novel, Mouchette then responds to her *voix intérieure*, like "an animal listens to his master as he encourages and pacifies him," by sliding into the water (1345). In the film, however, death seems to be imposed upon Mouchette *de l'extérieur* not only in the sections in which Bresson shows her as a victim of violence, but also by the symbolism of the hare massacre in the scene that precedes her death. During this final hunting scene, Bresson converts Bernanos' animal metaphors into images on the screen. According to P. Adams Sitney's formulation, in transposing these metaphors Bresson finds a "filmic substitution" for the access to interiority in the novel.[43]

Bresson not only refuses to reveal the heroine's inner thoughts, he also considerably alters the circumstances that surround Mouchette's drowning by filming her rolling down a slope three times.[44] In an interview with Ronald Hayman, Bresson affirmed his desire to stray from the literary text:

---

[42] Bresson's parallel structure then suggests that while Louisa can openly attend the fair with her lover, Mouchette's father prevents her (in a brutal manner) from simply talking to a boy.

[43] P. Adams Sitney, "Cinematography vs. the Cinema: Bresson's Figures," in *Robert Bresson*, James Quandt, ed. (Toronto: Cinémathèque Ontario, 1998), p. 149.

[44] Throughout the film, when Mouchette exits the frame to the left, she then re-enters from the right in the next shot, and vice versa. This method of filming her entrances and exits (in and out of the frame) prefigures Bresson's technical presentation of the suicide scene. In the first roll she exits the frame to the right and re-enters from the left, in the second she exits to the left and re-enters from the right, in the third she rolls out of the frame to the left and re-enters from the right, and then rolls out of the frame for the last time to the left.

> What shocked me in the book is that Bernanos makes her die by wanting to put her head in the water as if on her pillow in bed. I've never seen anyone committing suicide like that—waiting for death in the water.... When I read the book I immediately knew how the film should end: she should die by rolling downhill into the water.[45]

On screen, Mouchette's suicide appears almost accidental in that she plays a sort of game of a child rolling down a hill. Her descent begins innocently: she wraps the white muslin dress around herself as she rolls down the slope, and stops short of the water's edge. (Mouchette attempts to defile this "gift" from Philomène in the literary text, while in the film she tugs on the fabric after it has snagged on the branch of a shrub.) Then she hears the sound of a motor, marking the final aural manifestation of the menace already evoked by the (truck) motor motif. The heroine gets up and sees a man on his tractor to whom she waves, but the driver, after looking at her, continues on his way. His indifference suggests that if he, or any other villager, had paid attention to Mouchette, she would not continue her "game."

When Mouchette resumes the "game," the camera follows her with a series of panning shots. She climbs up to the top of the slope, and rolls down a second time through the crackling vegetation, more rapidly than the first. She again stops short of the water's edge, rolling into a bush, and walks back up the slope to roll down a third time. This time she rolls into the water.[46] Yet Bresson does not show the drowning. The camera follows only the beginning of the final movement of her life: she rolls down the embankment into and then out of the frame. Mouchette's body vanishes off-screen: without visible anguish or desperate gestures, the heroine simply disappears.[47] Next, we hear a splash; it is the sound of Mouchette's body entering the water off-screen.[48]

After the sound of her entry into the water, as Bresson holds the camera on the rings that ripple serenely across its surface until becoming smooth, we hear the *Magnificat* from the beginning of the film (from Monteverdi's *Vespers for the Blessed Virgin*).[49] Grace is present through this music,

---

[45] Ronald Hayman, "Robert Bresson in Conversation," *Transatlantic Review* 46 (1973), p. 21. Bresson told Georges Sadoul that he witnessed "several suicides [by drowning in the Seine] from his apartment on the Île Saint-Louis," in "Conversation plutôt qu'interview," p. 18.

[46] In Bernardo Bertolucci's *The Dreamers* (2003), the scene in which Isabelle, the heroine, attempts suicide is intercut with the suicide scene from *Mouchette*.

[47] The absence of her body recalls the absence of the curé's body, as well as Jesus' body on the cross, at the end of Bresson's *Journal d'un curé de campagne*.

[48] Her death is then expressed by means of sound, illustrating the importance of replacing images with sounds in accordance with Bresson's notion of the *cinématographe*.

[49] In 1936 (one year before *Nouvelle Histoire de Mouchette* was published) Bernanos claimed that *Journal d'un curé de campagne* was the only one of his books that he liked, and in describing the "failure" of his novel *La Joie* he claimed that the "awaited *Magnificat* never bursts out," in Albert Béguin's *Bernanos par lui-même*, p. 173. Perhaps Bresson was familiar with this comment.

suggesting Mouchette's salvation. Clearly the *Magnificat* is musical commentary: this song of joy responds to Mouchette's call for help, which is ignored by the man on the tractor, and represents a counterpoint to the violence of the heroine's world. In contrast to Mouchette's absence—her body vanishes off screen before it vanishes beneath the water—the music is spiritual presence.[50]

Bernanos asks God to grant his heroine mercy in the epigraph of the novel, and his plea/prayer for her salvation is then expressed through imagery as well as his *style de la tendresse*. According to Michel Estève, Mouchette is saved by God because the literary author evokes "the unsayable, the ineffable (*l'indicible*) of the sacred."[51] Bresson also concerns himself with the expression of *l'indicible* in comparing the notion of salvation in these two films: "In *Journal* God's name is pronounced on practically every page. In *Mouchette*, it never is—in this lies the difference. Only the language of the *cinématographe* allows [the spectator to] feel the effects of *l'indicible*."[52] Through *l'indicible* of the images and the feeling of redemption resounding from the *Magnificat*, Bresson suggests that Mouchette is saved in spite of her suicide—her salvation is implied through cinematic means. Like Bernanos, the filmmaker rejects the idea that Mouchette is a "hopeless case" in these comments on the final scene: "Since my film ends with a suicide, some see only despair.... This is not true for me because I believe in the soul and in God."[53] Bresson's script indicates that in rolling down the slope Mouchette's gaze is fixed on "the highest point in the sky," recalling the importance of that gaze in the novel.[54] In a discussion about the film, upon its release, Bresson neatly summarized the sense of the heroine's death: "this suicide is an attraction to Heaven."[55]

The filmmaker prepares the spectator for Mouchette's death: it is not a surprise because symbolic images and expressive sounds throughout the film indicate what will inevitably be the heroine's destiny.[56] From the very beginning of the film the mother's monologue creates an atmosphere of death and uneasiness. We then see the actual death of the partridges (in a scene that introduces Mouchette though she is absent), and along with Mouchette, we witness the mother's death as well as that of the hares. After the credits, the

---

[50] The *Magnificat* marks the last occurrence of non-diegetic music in Bresson's films.

[51] Michel Estève, *Bernanos: un triple itinéraire* (Paris: Hachette, 1981), p. 198.

[52] Robert Bresson, interview with Napoléon Murat in *Le Figaro littéraire*, March 16, 1967.

[53] Georges Sadoul, "Conversation plutôt qu'interview," p. 18.

[54] Robert Bresson, "*Mouchette*: découpage," p. 32.

[55] Robert Bresson, interview with Yvonne Baby in *Le Monde* November 11, 1971.

[56] Bresson does not, however, develop or emphasize the drowning motif in his film, as does Bernanos in the literary text.

partridge scene establishes an atmosphere of violence and cruelty, which Bresson presents in the rest of the film through the repetition of sounds and images.[57] Through Mouchette's suicide, however, Bresson transforms the cruelty against the heroine into liberation. The filmmaker claimed that although he needed to show that children can be the "victims of atrocious circumstances," the suicide scene exposes the "revelation" that Mouchette looks for in death.[58] This revelation is one of redemption and grace, suggested by the sound of church bells heard in the suicide scene.

Since Bresson films the suicide as a child playing a game, the viewer is invited to reflect on what her life has not been: we never see her at play with her peers, and her unique (positive) encounter with someone her age quickly turns into a scene of violence due to the father's intervention.[59] The sense of the heroine's suicide can then be found in the opening sections: one partridge dies, prefiguring the heroine's death, while another partridge is freed by the gamekeeper, revealing an image of liberation. Both partridges represent the heroine; her death and the liberation of her soul.

But how important is the element of chance in the suicide scene? The spectator has the impression that if the dress had not snagged on the branch of a shrub, or if the man on the tractor had responded to her wave, Mouchette would not die. It seems that Bresson chooses to show ambiguity through her two playful attempts at what could be suicide. The filmmaker presents parts of the suicide scene as a game of chance, as he explained to Ronald Hayman: "there are many ways of committing suicide and Russian roulette is one. Rolling downhill is a little girl's game, which is her equivalent."[60] The spectator may then view her death as an example of *hasard*.

The element of chance is absent from the novel, in which Mouchette dies less the victim of an indifferent and loveless village as the victim of her dreams. The heroine's death corresponds to the immense deception of her "great hope" and "marvelous expectation," both of which turn out to be illusions (1304). Since Bresson refuses any voice-over commentary that could reveal the heroine's inner thoughts, the spectator has to rely on images and sounds in the film to determine the sense of her death. The images of Mouchette making the sign of the cross with holy water—a suggestion of the baptismal quality of the pond in which she drowns—and the partridge flying

---

[57] Mouchette is both a victim of violence (the singing lesson, the fair scene, and the rape) and a witness to violence (the fight scene and the hare scene).

[58] Sadoul, "Conversation plutôt qu'interview," p. 18.

[59] In both the novel and the film, Mouchette is in a sense denied a childhood by her alcoholic father and dying mother. She also takes on adult responsibility in caring for both her mother and baby brother.

[60] Hayman, "Robert Bresson in Conversation," p. 17.

up to the sky imply her salvation.[61] The sound of the *Magnificat* then indicates the possibility of divine grace being extended even to a suicide; for a non-believer, it gives focus to a feeling of pity and compassion.

While Bernanos provides the reader access to his heroine's consciousness, there exists no filmic equivalent in *Mouchette* to the author-narrator's articulation of her mental processes. In *Journal d'un curé de campagne*, on the other hand, we have access to the curé's inner thoughts and feelings because the filmmaker transfers the diary form onto the screen. Bresson does so through the curé's act of writing and his voice-over narration. What is truly striking, then, is that Bresson transposes material from one of Bernanos' novels to his adaptation of a second Bernanos novel. For example, he re-states the motorcycle scene of *Journal d'un curé de campagne* in the bumper car scene of *Mouchette*: both episodes of happiness show the hero and heroine interacting with a companion their own age, and remind the spectator of their exclusion from the normal pleasures of youth. Another literary passage, in which Séraphita's father disrupts the moving encounter between his daughter and the curé (after his fall), is echoed in *Mouchette* when the father slaps his daughter at the fair, interrupting the positive interaction between Mouchette and the adolescent boy.

Though the numerous inventions in *Mouchette* expose Bresson's change in attitude concerning adaptation from one film to the other, both works illustrate the connection between *le cinématographe* and *l'indicible*. In both the literary and filmic texts, the curé's faith and Mouchette's salvation are notions of the "inexpressible." Bresson captures the "ineffable" in both films, to the extent that it possible through material means. Upon the release of *Mouchette*, Bresson pronounced these well-known words about his art: "the domain of the *cinématographe* is not only that of *l'indicible*, it is also the domain of *l'inexplicable*."[62]

---

[61] On the first Sunday in the film, the father violently shoves Mouchette as they enter the church so that she is propelled into the holy water font. While Bernanos explains that "no one goes to High Mass anymore," Bresson adds scenes in which characters are seen in or entering the church on both Sundays. Clearly Mouchette's contact with the holy water—implying her salvation—is the most significant element of these church scenes.

[62] Robert Bresson, interview with Yvonne Baby in *Le Monde*, March 14, 1967.

CONCLUSION

The preceding chapters have shown that Bresson's *Journal d'un curé de campagne* (1951) and *Mouchette* (1967) are autonomous works of art with their own integrity, even though the filmmaker was certainly inspired by the deep spirituality of the literary texts. Bernanos and Bresson try to touch God, though each in his own way, in accordance with the components of his own medium. Now I will consider Bresson's adaptations of Bernanos' novels in the context of his cinematic *œuvre*. In examining how his other films relate to *Journal d'un curé de campagne* and *Mouchette*, my focus will be on two topics, one technical and one substantive: Bresson's use of verbal narration and his presentation of suicide.

Verbal Narration

I have discussed the relation of images to spoken text in *Journal* through the various functions of the curé's voice-over, which repeatedly takes precedence over the visual rendering. Bresson employs voice-over narration in later films, specifically in *Un condamné à mort s'est échappé* (1956), *Pickpocket* (1959), and *Une femme douce* (1969). Like *Journal*, the first two of these works are first-person narratives in which the central character of the title dominates the film, and verbal narration allows us access to the hero's inner thoughts and perceptions. *Une femme douce*, on the other hand, differs from these first-person films because the heroine of the title is presented through the voice-over of another character, her husband.

In both *Un condamné à mort s'est échappé* and *Pickpocket*, Bresson reuses several functions of the curé's voice-over: the verbal narration of the protagonists, Fontaine and Michel, can precede, double, follow or replace visual enactment.[1] Within these functions, Bresson utilizes voice-over to convey the heroes' emotions (such as Fontaine's sadness and Michel's fear). The verbal narration then provides information about the heroes' state of mind, which the filmmaker omits from the visual rendering: we depend on the voice-over for a complete depiction of their emotional state.

In another parallel with *Journal*, Bresson chooses to emphasize voice-over narration by focusing on the heroes' faces, rather than on the object(s) of their gaze. In *Pickpocket*, for example, Michel explains in voice-over that his mother's face was calm as she slept. Bresson's camera then stays on the hero (refusing to show the mother), which recalls the curé's paying his last

---

[1] While Bresson employs voice-over narration in certain dialogue scenes of *Un condamné à mort s'est échappé* and *Pickpocket*, it never covers up the voices of others as in *Journal*.

respects to the countess. Furthermore, the verbal narration in *Pickpocket* contrasts at times with the visual depiction. When Michel contemplates stealing wallets in the subway, his voice-over explains that his hands were shaking, but we do not see them tremble in the visual rendering, as the hero's body simply sways with the movement of the train. In *Journal* when the curé's voice-over refers to his trembling during a period of spiritual crisis, the image of his body fails to reflect his anguish.

It is important to stress that Bresson employs both aural and written narration in *Pickpocket*. The first image of the film is a close-up shot of a hand writing in a diary, immediately recalling *Journal*, which is accompanied by the hero's reading of the entry in voice-over. Yet Bresson invents a written text for Michel without the references to God and movements of the soul that occupy the curé's diary (taken from Bernanos for the most part), nor the cross-outs that reflect his spiritual crisis. Additionally, in *Pickpocket* we lose the sense of the visuals being mediated by the act of writing. Voice-over narration is complemented by an image of Michel's diary merely four times in the film (only at the beginning of a scene or section), whereas in *Journal* Bresson continuously links the curé's voice-over with its source, the diary, so that off-screen narration always brings to mind the act of writing.

Suicide

Bresson based his first color film, *Une femme douce*, on Fyodor Dostoevsky's short story entitled "A Gentle Woman" (1876). The film-maker's change in attitude with regard to the adaptation of Bernanos' novels—he wanted to *servir le livre* for *Journal d'un curé de campagne* and *se servir* for *Mouchette*—also applies to the task of adapting Dostoevsky.[2] In order to *se servir*, Bresson starts by modernizing the story: he relocates the Russian couple from nineteenth-century St. Petersburg to contemporary Paris.

In both the novella and the film, the narrator is an unnamed pawnbroker who marries a destitute young woman (also nameless), and progressively encloses her with his will. In the preface, Dostoevsky writes: "Imagine a husband whose wife has committed suicide a few hours before by jumping out of the window.... He keeps pacing the room, trying to find some reason for what has happened.... So there he is, talking to himself, telling the whole story, trying to *explain* it to himself.[3]

---

[2] Robert Bresson, interview with Yvonne Baby in *Le Monde*, November 11, 1971.

[3] Fyodor Dostoevsky, "A Gentle Woman," in *The Short Stories of Dostoevsky*, William Phillips, ed. (New York: Dial Press, 1946), p. 261.

The husband in the film, on the other hand, has a direct interlocutor, Anna the elderly housekeeper (Lukerya of the novella). Bresson alternates present scenes of the despairing husband pacing around his wife's corpse with past scenes of the couple, which are frequently linked by the sound of his voice-over narration and his footsteps. The dialectic between present and past is doubled by that of life and death: in every return to the past, the husband recalls a different incident with his wife, and in every return to the present, Bresson's camera frames a different angle of her corpse on the bed.

Une femme douce opens and closes with the wife's suicide, marking the only time that Bresson presents death at the beginning of a film. While the novella starts with the husband's description of his wife's lifeless body stretched out over two card tables, Bresson begins the film by showing how the death occurred so that, in his own words, the "effect precedes the cause."[4] The first four shots of *Une femme douce* are quick and riveting: a close-up of the handle of a glass-paned door, which is opened by an elderly woman, a medium long shot of a balcony where a chair jerks back violently, a table falls over, and a flower pot shatters, a long shot of a white shawl floating from the balcony, and finally, a medium shot of the body of a young woman lying face down on the sidewalk with blood streaming from her head.

Bresson refuses to give any establishing shots or explanation for what just happened (recalling the opening sections of *Mouchette*). Instead of presenting the violence of the suicide—the wife jumps off-screen—Bresson suggests the act through its physical effects: a table falling, a chair rocking, a scarf floating, and a head bleeding. Sounds also suggest the act: we hear the plant and table crashing down, cars screeching to a halt, and a siren wailing. Bresson denies our access to the subject of the action, focusing instead on visual details so that the plant, table, and shawl imitate her descent. As in *Mouchette*, Bresson's selection of means used to present the wife's suicide creates, as Lee Atwell argues, "a deeper impression than a direct, literal description."[5]

Throughout *Une femme douce*, the husband attempts to discover why his wife committed suicide, but cannot find an answer—nor can the spectator. As usual Bresson refuses psychological explanation, presenting the suicide (twice) rather than explaining it. Both *Mouchette* and *Une femme douce* are marked by the absence of psychological detail and motivation: the mental acts or states that bring about the suicide of the title characters are not clarified. Bresson rarely explains; rather, he intimates. For example, the husband and wife watch a scene from *Hamlet*, featuring the duel between Hamlet and Laertes (V, 2). By showing this scene of the play (which is

---

[4] Robert Bresson, *Notes sur le cinématographe*, p. 102.
[5] Lee Atwell, *"Une femme douce,"* *Film Quarterly* 23 (Summer 1970), p. 55.

absent from the novella), Bresson reminds us of the whole play, in particular of Hamlet's famous contemplation of suicide: "To be or not to be" (III, 1).[6]

Like the opening scene of the film, Bresson's presentation of the wife's suicide at the end is not mediated by the husband's voice-over narration: the filmmaker places the spectator in Anna's position for a second time. (The fact that the husband does not witness the suicide compounds the futility of his attempt to understand her act.) In the last scene, Bresson focuses on the significant actions that immediately precede the wife's death: she gently caresses a gold-mounted crucifix, puts on the white shawl, and smiles at herself in the mirror (an object added by Bresson) in a gesture of resignation. In the novella, Lukerya informs the husband that his wife took out her "icon of the Holy Mother" and that she seemed "to be praying to it" before leaping to her death clutching that icon.[7] Bresson *replaces* the icon with the white shawl and the wife's gesture of wrapping it around herself suggests a shroud, recalling Mouchette's white muslin dress.

The last time we see the wife's face, Bresson frames her eyes in an extreme close-up—the only one in the film—from behind the glass-paned door. She then opens the door and exits the frame to leap to her death. Again we see the table and plant crashing down, and hear the screeching sound of car brakes and the wail of a siren. Bresson refuses to show the wife's descent for a second time; instead he films the white shawl suspended in air to avoid, in his own words, "the cliché of showing the wife falling to the pavement."[8] The shawl then floats down after the wife, not with her, as she falls to her death. Rather than show the sidewalk again, Bresson cuts to an image of the wife's open coffin. The husband lifts up her head to tell her in his final desperate quest for understanding: "Open your eyes for a second, just a second."[9] Then the undertaker slides the lid onto the coffin, and begins screwing the bolts into the wood. The final sound we hear in the film is the dreadful grating of the screws, as opposed to the *Magnificat*.

In Bresson's *Le Diable probablement* (1977), Charles, a young student, is fixed on taking his own life.[10] Disgusted with the social, ecological, and

---

[6] The husband attempts to explain his wife's death in the following passage of the literary text: "It must have been because she was frightened by my amorousness—because she asked herself seriously, 'To consent or not to consent?' and, unable to face the problem, preferred death," in Dostoevsky's *Short Stories*, p. 315. It is interesting to note that, in addition to theater, Bresson also shows clips from a film (Michel Deville's *Benjamin* released in 1968) and from television for the first time in *Une femme douce*.

[7] Dostoevsky, *Short Stories*, p. 313.

[8] Charles Samuels, *Encountering Directors*, p. 74.

[9] This line comes from the husband's interior monologue at the end of the novella.

[10] Bresson shows this fixation, for example, when Charles steps out of the bathtub after attempting suicide. The hero tells the young woman who was knocking on the bathroom door, "You can't put your head at the bottom of the water and just wait." These words recall Bresson's comments

political horror of our world, he quotes *The Brothers Karamazov* in his math book: "When will I kill myself, if not now?" Yet instead of killing himself directly, Charles hires a junkie named Valentin to shoot him.[11] Right after the credits we see two editions of a newspaper with the following headlines: "A Young Man Kills Himself at Père-Lachaise / The Suicide at Père-Lachaise was a Homicide." This incongruity is explained in the final scene of the film: although Valentin leaves the gun in Charles' hand to make the death appear self-inflicted, he neglects to wipe his own fingerprints off the gun.

Seconds before his death, Charles utters these words to Valentin in the cemetery: "At such a solemn moment, I thought I'd have sublime thoughts." His next statement—"want me to tell you what I was..."—is cut short by the sound of a gunshot: we see Valentin pull the trigger. He then approaches Charles' body, places the gun in the victim's hand, takes money out of his pocket, and walks away. Bresson makes it clear that the young hero (like the wife) finds neither salvation nor grace in death. Earlier in the film, when his psychologist asks Charles if he believes in God, the young man responds: "I believe in eternal life as much as I can. But if I take my own life, I can't imagine that God would judge me for not understanding the incomprehensible." Charles fails to find redemption in religion, revolution or love, as the title itself suggests the pessimistic outcome of the film.[12]

Bresson's turn to pessimism begins with *Une femme douce* (released only two years after *Mouchette*) in that he refuses a salvific ending. All of his films that follow *Mouchette* are in color, not in black and white. This change marks a ironic contrast between somber visuals (his black and white films) and somber messages (his color films). Bresson undoubtedly suggests Mouchette's salvation through Monteverdi's *Magnificat*: this sacred song of joy and spiritual triumph stands in counterpoint to the various forms of violence and misery in the heroine's life.[13] In *Mouchette* the possibility of divine grace extends to a young girl's suicide, and redemption becomes, in Bresson's formulation, the "revelation" that the heroine seeks in death.[14]

While in *Mouchette* the music signals God's mercy, there is no such sign in *Une femme douce*: the wife's death lacks a sense of hope, comfort or

---

about the way in which Bernanos depicted Mouchette's suicide.

[11] The idea of hiring Valentin is suggested to Charles by his psychologist, who tells the hero that ancient Romans contemplating suicide often hired their own executioners.

[12] Although the title comes from Dostoevsky's *The Brothers Karamazov*, *Le Diable probablement* is Bresson's most original script. (Charles hears the title phrase when he is riding a bus: one of the passengers asks, "Who is controlling us on the sly?" and another replies, "The devil probably." After this response, the bus collides with another vehicle.)

[13] Although in *Le Diable probablement* Charles and Valentin listen to Monteverdi's *Ego Dormio* on a record player in the St. Eustache church, Valentin then breaks open and steals money from the offertory boxes—clearly Bresson refuses a salvific message.

[14] Georges Sadoul, "Conversation plutôt qu'interview, p. 18.

salvation. At first the shot of the floating scarf may evoke the flight of partridges in *Mouchette* and the doves that fly from Joan of Arc's pyre (in Bresson's *Procès de Jeanne d'Arc*, released in 1962). Yet the death of these two heroines suggests that their souls "fly up" in the sense of divine liberation, whereas the heavy lid of the coffin closes on the wife's body. In *Une femme douce* Bresson eliminates practically any spiritual or religious context, contrary to all of his films that precede it. The curé and Joan of Arc (as well as Fontaine and Michel) participate in a spiritual journey, and like Mouchette, they experience a spiritual liberation at the end of the film.

Despite physical or spiritual confinement, the possibility of redemption and grace in Bresson's films before *Une femme douce* is summed up in the curé's last words, *tout est grâce*. These words resonate with powerful tones through the death of the title characters in *Procès de Jeanne d'Arc*, *Au hasard Balthazar*, and *Mouchette*, though each has its own recognition. (Balthazar the donkey dies among a flock of sheep, recalling the gospel of John: "The good shepherd lays down his life for the sheep.") Starting with *Une femme douce*, the central character in Bresson's films no longer finds spiritual redemption through grace. The filmmaker never touches Bernanos again: perhaps one could say that *Une femme douce* quite clearly marks the end of the Bernanosian phase of Bresson's cinematic *œuvre*.

Both of Bernanos' novels, *Journal d'un curé de campagne* (1936) and *Nouvelle Histoire de Mouchette* (1937), breathe his yearning for a spiritual meaning in life, attained through *Sainte Agonie* (which is multilayered: Human Agony in general, Jesus' Agony on the Cross, and through it even a "personification," *Saint Agony*). Bernanos did not write any (new) novels after *Nouvelle Histoire de Mouchette*—feeling compelled to flee from Fascism and World War II to South America, where he passionately wrote against Nazism and the collaborative Pétain French government. Nevertheless, after returning to post-war France, he turned one last time to fiction writing.[15]

In 1947, Father Raymond Bruckberger was working on a film script based on Gertrud von le Fort's novel, *Die Letzte am Schafott* (*The Song at the Scaffold*, published in 1931), and asked Bernanos to write the dialogue. In what would become a stage version, Bernanos rediscovered the themes of agony and grace, death and salvation in his *Dialogues des Carmélites*.[16]

[15] In 1940, Bernanos finished the last pages of his novel *Monsieur Ouine*, which he had started in 1931. This work was published in 1943.

[16] In 1949, Bernanos' editor and literary executor Albert Béguin published the script as a play and gave it the title. In this text (which Bernanos finished three months before his death in 1948) Blanche declares: "There was always only one morning...that of Easter. But every night we enter is that of the most *Sainte Agonie*" (1575). In Gaëton Picon's preface to Bernanos' *Œuvres romanesques, suivies de Dialogues des Carmélites*, it is noted that just hours before he died, Bernanos himself declared: *Je suis pris dans la Sainte Agonie* (p. xvii).

Ultimately, in 1957, this work became the libretto for Francis Poulenc's opera of the same name—it too portrayed salvation coming through *Sainte Agonie*, as the heroine, after running away, returns to share with her fellow Carmelite sisters the fate of the guillotine just ten days before Robespierre himself was consumed by the Terror he had unleashed, thereby quenching it.[17]

Thus Bernanos continued to the end to find spiritual meaning in life and in his writing. But this seemingly was not true for Bresson, or if it was, it was opaquely so. After *Mouchette* (1967), the deaths of his heroes/heroines are marked by meaningless agony. Given that he so effectively grasped the "pearl" of salvation in the Bernanos films, it is striking that just two years after *Mouchette* he made *Une femme douce* wherein the heroine leaps to her death and no redeeming music or gesture plucks the victim or viewer back from the abyss. In stark contrast to Bernanos—for whom *tout est grâce* indicates the end of *Sainte Agonie*—the *femme douce* appears simply to succumb to an unredeeming *coup de grâce*.

---

[17] Poulenc then inherited a text composed in three forms: novel, script, and play. Bruckberger, along with Philippe Agostini, finally made the film in 1960, giving it a new title, *Le Dialogue des Carmélites*.

BIBLIOGRAPHY

Primary Sources—Bernanos and Bresson

Bernanos, Georges. *Correspondance inédite. Combat pour la vérité* (volume I). *Combat pour la liberté* (volume II). Paris: Plon, 1971.

——. *Essais et écrits de combat.* Paris: Gallimard, 1971.

——. *Les Grands Cimetières sous la lune.* Paris: Plon, 1962.

——. *Œuvres romanesques, suivies de Dialogues des Carmélites.* Bibliothèque de la Pléiade. Paris: Gallimard, 1961.

Bresson, Robert. "*Mouchette*: découpage." *L'Avant-scène* 80 (1968): 5–32.

——. *Notes sur le cinématographe.* Paris: Gallimard, 1975.

——. "Propos." *Cahiers du cinéma* 75 (October 1957): 3–9.

——. "Une mise en scène n'est pas un art." *Cahiers du cinéma* 543 (February 2000): 4–11.

Journal d'un curé de campagne. Dir. Robert Bresson. Perf. Claude Laydu, Jean Riveyre, Armand Guilbert, Nicole Ladmiral, and Marie-Monique Arkell. Union Générale Cinématographique, 1951.

Le Diable probablement. Dir. Robert Bresson. Perf. Antoine Monnier, Tina Irrisari, Henri de Maublanc, Laetitia Carcano, and Nicolas Deguy. Sunchild GMF, 1977.

Mouchette. Dir. Robert Bresson. Perf. Nadine Nortier, Marie Cardinal, Paul Hébert, Jean-Claude Guilbert, and Jean Vimenet. Argos Films, 1967.

Pickpocket. Dir. Robert Bresson. Perf. Martin Lassalle, Pierre Leymarie, Jean Pélégri, and Marika Green. Agnès Delahaie, 1959.

Un condamné à mort s'est échappé. Dir. Robert Bresson. Perf. François Leterrier, Charles Le Clainche, Rolond Monod, and Jacques Ertaud. Gaumont, 1956.

Une femme douce. Dir. Robert Bresson. Perf. Dominique Sanda, Guy Frangin, Jane Lobre, and Claude Ollier. Parc Film, 1969.

Secondary Sources—Bernanos

Aaraas, Hans. *A propos de Journal d'un curé de campagne: essai sur l'écrivain et le prêtre dans l'œuvre romanesque de Bernanos.* Paris: Lettres Modernes, 1966.

——. "Bernanos in 1988." *Renascence* 51 (Fall 1988): 15–28.

——. *Littérature et sacerdoce: essai sur Journal d'un curé de campagne de Bernanos.* Paris: Lettres Modernes, 1984.

Balthasar, Hans Urs von. *Le Chrétien Bernanos.* Paris: Seuil, 1957.

Beaumont, Ernest. "Le Sens christique de l'œuvre romanesque de Bernanos." *Études bernanosiennes* 3–4 (1963): 85–106.

——. "Structure et symboles." *Études bernanosiennes* 9 (1968): 5–30.

Béguin, Albert. "Bernanos au cinéma." *Esprit* (February 1951): 248–252.

——. *Bernanos par lui-même.* Paris: Éditions du Seuil, 1954.

Berthe, Claude. "Bernanos, la peur ou l'insondable de Dieu." *Travaux de littérature* 16 (2003): 105–121.

Bridel, Yves. *Esprit d'enfance dans l'œuvre romanesque de Georges Bernanos.* Paris: Minard, 1966.

Bush, William. *Souffrance et expiation dans la pensée de Bernanos.* Paris: Minard, 1962.

Chabot, Jacques. "Chronologie et liturgie dans le *Journal d'un curé de campagne.*" *Revue des Sciences Humaines* 207 (July–September 1987): 111–119.

Chao, Denise W. *Le Style du Journal d'un curé de campagne*. Washington: University Press of America, 1981.

Chéry-Aynesworth, Janine. *Approche rhétorique de la dialecte des sens chez Bernanos*. Paris: Minard, 1983.

Comfort, Kathy. "Imperiled Souls: Metaphorical Representations of Spiritual Confusion in Bernanos's *Journal d'un curé de campagne*." *Renascence* 57 (Fall 2004): 29–46.

Cor, Lawrence. "Mystical Perception in *Journal*." *Romance Notes* 12 (Spring 1971): 244–250.

Estève, Michel, ed. "Autour de 'Nouvelle Histoire de Mouchette.'" *Études bernanosiennes* 22 (2001): 1–223.

———. *Bernanos*. Paris: Gallimard, 1965.

———. *Bernanos et la modernité*. Paris: Minard, 1998.

———. *Bernanos: un triple itinéraire*. Paris: Hachette, 1981.

———. "Genèse du *Journal d'un curé de campagne*." *Études bernanosiennes* 2 (1961–1962): 3–17.

———. "La Nuit de Gethsémani." *Études bernanosiennes* 18 (1986): 87–108.

———. *Le Sens de l'amour dans les romans de Bernanos*. Paris: Minard, 1961.

Fitch, Brian T. *Dimensions et structures chez Bernanos*. Paris: Lettres Modernes, 1969.

———. "Vide mental et structure en creux dans *Journal d'un curé de campagne*." *Courier Georges Bernanos* 2–4 (February 1971): 40–52.

Fitting, Peter. "Narrateur et narration." *Études bernanosiennes* 9 (1968): 55–80.

Flower, John Ernest. *Georges Bernanos: Journal d'un curé de campagne*. London: Edward Arnold, 1970.

———. "The *Comtesse* episode in the *Journal d'un curé de campagne*." *The French Review* 42 (1969): 673–682.

Garda, Claude. "La Nuit dans *Journal d'un curé de campagne*." *Études bernanosiennes* 18 (1986): 57–86.

Gaucher, Guy. *Le Thème de la mort dans les romans de Georges Bernanos*. Paris: Minard, 1967.

Giordon, Henri. "La Réalité sociale et politique dans le *Journal d'un Curé de campagne*." *Études bernanosiennes* 2 (1961–1962): 85–122.

Gosselin, Monique. "La Parole et le corps dans *Journal d'un curé de campagne*." *Revue des Sciences Humaines* 207 (July–September 1987): 90–110.

Heyer, Astrid. *La Femme dans le monde imaginaire de Georges Bernanos*. New York: Peter Lang, 1999.

Hoffbeck, Gérard. *Journal d'un curé de campagne de Bernanos*. Paris: Hachette, 1972.

Howe, Fanny. "Au Hasard Suicide." *Brick* 71 (Summer 2003): 44–53.

Hubert, Etienne-Alain. "L'Expression romanesque du surnaturel dans le *Journal d'un curé de campagne*." *Études bernanosiennes* 2 (1961–1962): 17–55.

Kidd, Marilyn. "Les Miroirs et l'importance du reflet dans les romans de Bernanos." *Études bernanosiennes* 19 (1988): 143–157.

Kushnir, Slava M. *Le Héros et son double: essai sur le Journal d'un curé de campagne de Georges Bernanos*. Sherbrooke: Naaman, 1984.

Le Touzé, Philippe. "Aspects de la communication dans *Journal d'un curé de campagne* de Bernanos." *Revue des sciences humaines* 207 (July–September 1987): 79–89.

———. *Le Mystère du reel dans les romans de Bernanos*. Paris: Nizet, 1979.

Lye, John. "*The Diary of a Country Priest* and the Christian Novel." *Renascence* 30 (1978): 19–31.

Marie-Céleste, Sœur. *Bernanos et son optique de la vie chrétienne*. Paris: Nizet, 1967.

———. *Le Sens de l'agonie dans l'œuvre de Georges Bernanos*. Paris: P. Lethielleux, 1962.

McNamee, John P. *Diary of a City Priest*. Kansas City: Sheed and Ward, 1993.

Mesnier, Pierre. *Univers imaginaire et poétique du surnaturel dans Nouvelle Histoire de Mouchette de Bernanos.* Paris: Minard, 1974.

Milner, Max. *Georges Bernanos.* Paris: Desclée de Brouwer, 1967.

Nettlebeck, Colin W. *Les Personnages de Bernanos romancier.* Paris: Minard, 1970.

Not, André. *Les Dialogues dans l'œuvre de Bernanos.* Toulouse: Éditions Universitaires du Sud, 1990.

O'Sharkey, Eithne. *The Role of the Priest in the Novels of Georges Bernanos.* New York: Vantage Press, 1983.

Peeters, Leopold. "Narration et tendresse dans *Nouvelle Histoire de Mouchette.*" *Études bernanosiennes* 17 (1982): 145–159.

———. *Une prose du monde: essai sur le langage de l'adhésion dans l'œuvre de Bernanos.* Paris: Minard, 1984.

Pénicaud, Anne. "Approches de la vision bernanosienne de la pauvreté." *Études bernanosiennes* 18 (1986): 109–132.

Pleau, Jean-Christian. *Bernanos: la part obscure.* New York: Peter Lang, 1998.

Poulet, Georges. *Le Point de départ.* Paris: Plon, 1964.

Raoul, Valérie. "Narcisse prêtre: reflets ambigus dans *Journal d'un curé de campagne.*" *Texte* 1 (1982): 97–109.

Rechou, Romain. "Note sur le procédé du journal intime." *Études bernanosiennes* 18 (1986): 33–42.

Renard-Georges, Pierrette. "Métamorphoses et spiritualité du paysage." *Études bernanosiennes* 9 (1968): 31–54.

———. "Bernanos et Bresson." *Études bernanosiennes* 9 (1968): 81–106.

Renaud, Gaston. "Vision décléricalisée: Chantal de Clergerie et le Curé d'Ambricourt." *Courier Georges Bernanos* 2–4 (February 1971): 65–77.

Rivas, Daniel. "A propos du temps et de la création dans le *Journal d'un curé de campagne.*" *Studi Francesi* 71 (May–August 1980): 289–294.

Storelv, Sven. "A propos du thème du mal chez Bernanos." *Études bernanosiennes* 9 (1968): 200–206.

Stubbs, Marcelle. "Mythe exemplaire et récit réactualisé." *Études bernanosiennes* 19 (1988): 81–111.

Vineberg, Elsa. "*Journal d'un curé de campagne*: A Psychoanalytic reading." *Modern Language Notes* 92 (1977): 825–829.

Whitehouse, John C. "La Protestation du mystère." *Études bernanosiennes* 19 (1988): 157–190.

Winter, Nicole. "Conception bernanosienne du sacerdoce à partir du *Journal d'un curé de campagne.*" *Études bernanosiennes* 2 (1961–1962): 55–85.

Yücel, Tashin. "Dialogues du curé d'Ambricourt: le temps, l'espace, et l'être." *Études bernanosiennes* 18 (1986): 17–32.

Secondary Sources—Bresson

Affron, Mirella Jona. "Bresson and Pascal: Rhetorical Affinities." *Quarterly Review of Film Studies* 10 (Spring 1985): 118–134.

Agel, Henri. *Le Cinéma et le sacré.* Paris: Editions du Cerf, 1961.

———. "Présentation de Robert Bresson." *Études* (May 1957): 263–269.

Ajame, Pierre. "Le Cinéma selon Bresson." *Les Nouvelles littéraires* 260 (May 1966): 13.

Amiel, Vincent. *Le Corps au cinéma: Keats, Bresson, Cassavetes.* Paris: Presses Universitaires de France, 1998.

Andrews, Dudley. "Desperation and Meditation: Bresson's *Diary of a Country Priest.*" In *Modern European Filmmakers and the Art of Adaptation,* edited by Andrew Horton, 20–37. New York: Ungar, 1981.

————. "The Past and the Passing of Death in French Cinema." *L'Esprit créateur* 35 (Winter 1995): 7–17.

Arnaud, Philippe. *Robert Bresson*. Paris: Cahiers du Cinéma, 1986.

Arnault, Hubert. "Apparence de Robert Bresson: entretien avec Jean Vimenet." *Image et son* 210 (November 1967): 58–72.

Astre, Georges-Albert. "Entretien avec Robert Bresson et Jean Guitton." *Études cinématographiques* 18–19 (Fall 1962): 85–97.

Atwell, Lee. "*Une femme douce*." *Film Quarterly* 23 (Summer 1970): 54–56.

Ayfre, Amédée. *Dieu au cinéma: problèmes esthétiques du film religieux*. Paris: Presses Universitaires de France, 1953.

————. "L'Univers de Robert Bresson." *Téléciné* 70–71 (November–December 1957): 1–8.

Baby, Yvonne. "L'Art n'est pas un luxe mais un besoin vital." *Le Monde*, November 11, 1971: 13.

————. "Le Domaine de l'indicble." *Le Monde*, March 14, 1967: 24.

————. "Du fer qui fait du bruit." *Le Monde*, December 26, 1974: 15.

————. "Entretien avec Robert Bresson: *Procès de Jeanne d'Arc*." *Le Monde*, March 16, 1963: 24.

Baroncelli, Jean. "Le Cinéma: *Mouchette* de Bresson." *Le Monde*, March 14, 1967: 24.

Bastaire, Jean. "Petite introduction à Robert Bresson." *Esprit* 95 (March 1960): 565–577.

Bazin, André. "Le *Journal d'un curé de campagne* et la stylistique de Robert Bresson." *Cahiers du cinéma* 3 (June 1951): 7–22.

————. *Qu'est-ce le cinéma?* Paris: Cerf, 1975.

————. "*Un condamné à mort s'est échappé*." *France-Observateur* 340 (November 1956): 22–23.

Béguin, Albert. "L'Adaptation du *Journal d'un curé de campagne*." *Glanes* 18 (May 1951): 24–28.

Benayoun, Robert. "En trois personnes." *Positif* 85 (June 1967): 49–52.

Ben-Gad, Schmuel. "To See the World Profoundly: The Films of Robert Bresson." *Cross Currents* (Summer 1997): 230–235.

Bertin, Celia. "Cinéma: une écriture avec des images et des sons." *La Revue de Paris* 74 (May1967): 139–141.

Billard, Pierre. "*Cinéma 63* remet en question Robert Bresson." *Cinéma 63* 73 (February 1963): 13–33.

————. "Un pur chef-d'œuvre sous le soleil de Satan." *L'Express* (March 1967): 60–61.

Bonnaud, Frederic. "*Diary of a Country Priest*." *Film Comment* 35 (May–June 1999): 41–44.

Briot, René. *Robert Bresson*. Paris: Éditions du Cerf, 1957.

Browne, Nick. "Film Form/Voice-Over: Bresson's *Diary of a Country Priest*." *Yale French Studies* 60 (1980): 233–240.

Burch, Noël and Geneviève Sellier. *La 'Drôle de guerre' des sexes du cinéma français 1930–1956*. Paris: Éditions Nathan, 1996.

Cardinal, Marie. *Cet été-là*. Paris: Nouvelles Éditions Oswald, 1979.

Capendac, Michel. "J'ai voulu que Jeanne d'Arc soit un personnage d'aujourd'hui." *Les Lettres françaises* 928 (May 1962): 12.

Chabot, Jacques. "L'Accueil de la critique en 1937 et 1967." *Études bernanosiennes* 9 (1968): 109–180.

Chapier, Henri. "*Mouchette* de Robert Bresson." *Combat* 41 (March 1967): 8.

Charensol, Georges. "Le Cinéma: *Journal d'un curé de campagne*." *Les Nouvelles littéraires* 123 (Febraury 1951): 8.

————. "Signes: *Mouchette* par Robert Bresson." *Les Nouvelles littéraires* 263 (March 1967): 14.

Ciment, Michel. "Je ne cherche pas une description mais une vision des choses: entretien avec Robert Bresson autour de *L'Argent*." *Positif* 430 (December 1996): 93–101.

Cunneen, Joseph. *Robert Bresson: A Spiritual Style in Film*. New York: Continuum, 2003.

Dadoun, Roger. "Bilan de Bresson." *La Quinzaine littéraire* (April 1967): 28.

Daney, Serge. "Rencontre avec Robert Bresson: mise au point à propos de *La Genèse*." *Cahiers du cinéma* 22 (March 1982): 7.

———. "Entretien avec Robert Bresson." *Cahiers du cinéma* 346 (June–July 1983): 13–14.

Deluze, Gilles. *Cinéma II: l'image-temps*. Paris: Minuit, 1985.

Dempsey, Michael. "Despair Abounding: The Recent Films of Robert Bresson." *Film Quarterly* 34 (1980): 2–14.

Doniol-Valcroze, Jacques and Jean-Luc Godard. "Entretien avec Robert Bresson." *Cahiers du cinéma* 104 (February 1960): 3–9.

Dorsky, Nathaniel. *Devotional Cinema*. Berkeley: Tuumba Press, 2003.

Douchet, Jean. "Bresson on location." *Sequence* 13 (January 1951): 6–8.

Droguet, Robert. "Robert Bresson." *Premier plan* 42 (November 1966): 4–89.

Duca, Lo. "Un acte de foi." *Cahiers du cinéma* 1 (April 1951): 45–47.

Durgnat, Raymond. "Le *Journal d'un curé de campagne*." In *The Films of Robert Bresson*, edited by Ian Cameron, 42–50. New York: Praeger, 1969.

Estève, Michel. "Bernanos et Bresson: étude de *Journal d'un curé de campagne* et *Mouchette*." *Archives Bernanos* 7 (1978): 33–111.

———. "De Bernanos à Bresson." *Esprit* 360 (May 1967): 925–929.

———. "De *Nouvelle Histoire de Mouchette* à *Mouchette*." *L'Esprit créateur* 8 (Winter 1968): 268–283.

———. *Robert Bresson*. Paris: Editions Seghers, 1962.

———. *Robert Bresson: la passion du cinématographe*. Paris: Éditions Albatros, 1983.

Fennec, Claude. "Mère sainte Bob." *Arts-loisirs* (March 1967): 24–26.

Fieschi, Jean. "Robert Bresson." *Cinématographe* 29 (July 1977): 28–30.

Feldman, Ellen. "Bresson's Adaptation of Bernanos' *The Diary of a Country Priest*." *West Virginia Philological Papers* 26 (August 1980): 37–42.

Fraser, Peter. *Images of the Passion: The Sacramental Mode in Film*. Westport: Praeger, 1998.

Gardies, René. "*Mouchette*." *Image et son* 207 (May 1967): 145–147.

Gerlach, John. "*The Diary of a Country Priest*: A Total Conversion." *Literature/Film Quarterly* 4 (Winter 1976): 39–45.

Godard, Jean-Luc and Michel Delahaye. "La Question: entretien avec Robert Bresson." *Cahiers du cinéma* 178 (May 1966): 26–35.

Greene, Marjorie. "Robert Bresson." *Film Quarterly* 13 (Spring 1960): 5–10.

Hanlon, Lindley. *Fragments: Bresson's Film Style*. Rutherford: Farleigh Dickinson University Press, 1986.

———. "Sound in Bresson's *Mouchette*." In *Film Sound: Theory and Practice*, edited by John Belton, 323–331. New York: Columbia University Press, 1985.

Hayman, Ronald. "Robert Bresson in Conversation with Donald Hayman." *Transatlantic Review* 46–47 (1973): 16–23.

Herpe, Noël. "Bresson dans le temps." *Positif* 430 (December 1996): 76–78.

Hess, John. "*La Politique des auteurs*, Part One: World View as Aesthetic." *Jump Cut* 1 (May–June 1974): 19–22.

———. "*La Politique des auteurs*, Part Two: Truffaut's Manifesto." *Jump Cut* 2 (July–August 1974): 20–22.

Hourigan, Jonathan. "On Two Deaths and Three Births: The Cinematography of Robert Bresson." *Stills* I (Autumn 1981): 27–38.

Jacob, Gilles. "*Mouchette* de Robert Bresson." *Cinéma* 116 (May 1967): 50–59.

Kébadian, Jacques. "Éloge de la sensation." *Cahiers du cinéma* 543 (February 2000): 18–20.

Kovacs, Yves. "Entretien avec Robert Bresson." *Cahiers du cinéma* 140 (February 1963): 4–9.

Labarthe, André S. "La Cybernétique de Robert Bresson." *Cahiers du cinéma* 189 (April 1967): 63–64.

Lacroix, Jean. "Vie intérieure et vie spirituelle." *Le Monde*, May 15, 1954: 9.

Lambert, Gavin. "Notes on Robert Bresson." *Sight and Sound* 23 (July–September 1953): 35–39.

Latil Le Dantec, Mireille. "Bresson, Dostoïevski." *Cinématographe* 73 (1981): 25–39.

———. "Du cinéma au 'cinématographe.'" *Études* 387 (December 1997): 667–676.

Lopate, Phillip. "Films as Spiritual Life." *Film Comment* 27 (November 1991): 26–30.

———. "*Mouchette.*" *Film Comment* 35 (May–June 1999): 55–58.

Machuel, Emmanuel. "Ce que l'on voit dans la caméra." *Cahiers du cinéma* 543 (February 2000): 15–17.

Magnan, Henry. "Le *Journal d'un curé de campagne* marquera une date dans l'histoire du cinéma." *Le Monde*, February 8, 1951: 8.

Magny, Joël. "L'Expérience intérieure de Robert Bresson." *Cinéma* 294 (June 1983): 19–26.

Marion, Denis. "Petit journal intime du cinéma." *Cahiers du cinéma* 36 (June 1954): 45.

Mauriac, Claude. "Le Premier film de la vie intérieure." *Le Figaro littéraire* 251 (February 1951): 15.

Mauriac, François. "*Journal d'un curé de campagne.*" *Le Figaro*, February 27, 1951: 1.

McNeece, Lucy Stone. "Bresson's 'Miracle' of the Flesh: *Mouchette.*" *The French Review* 65 (1991): 276–279.

Michelson, Annette. "Etc." *Commonweal* 29 (November 1968): 318–319.

Milne, Tom. "*Mouchette.*" *Sight and Sound* 37 (Summer 1968): 152–153.

Monod, Roland. "En travaillant avec Robert Bresson." *Cahiers du cinéma* 64 (November 1956): 16–20.

Murat, Napoléon. "Bresson s'explique sur son nouveau film." *Le Figaro littéraire* (March 1967): 3.

Oms, Marcel. "Quatre Bernanos au cinéma: la grâce sous la braise." *CinémAction* 49 (October 1988): 89–93.

Oudart, Jean-Pierre. "Le Hors-champ de l'auteur." *Cahiers du cinéma* 236–237 (March 1972): 86–89.

Papin, Liliane. "Film et écriture du silence: de Chaplin à Duras." *Stanford French Review* 13 (1989): 211–228.

Pauly, Rebecca. *The Transparent Illusion: Image and Ideology in French Text and Film.* New York: Peter Lang, 1993.

Petrie, Graham. "*Mouchette.*" *Film Quarterly* 22 (Fall 1968): 52–56.

Pézeril, Daniel. "Mouchette entre Bernanos et Bresson." *Les Nouvelles littéraires* 263 (March 1967): 3.

Pinel, Vincent. "Le Paradoxe du non-comédien." *Études cinématographiques* 14 (January–March 1962): 78–84.

Polet, Jacques. "Bernanos à l'écran." *Les Lettres romanes* 42 (November 1988): 443–456.

Polhemus, Helen M. "Matter and Spirit in the Films of Robert Bresson." *Film Heritage* 9 (Spring 1974): 12–16.

Prédal, René. "Robert Bresson: l'aventure intérieure." *L'Avant-scène* 408–409 (January 1992): 3–37.

Quandt, James, ed. *Robert Bresson.* Toronto: Cinémathèque Ontario, 1998.

Rancière, Jacques. "La Voix de Séraphita." *Cahiers du cinéma* 543 (February 2000): 27–30.

Reader, Keith. "D'où cela vient-il?: Notes on Three Films by Robert Bresson." *French Studies* 40 (April 1986): 427–442.

————. *Robert Bresson*. Manchester: Manchester University Press, 2000.

————. "The Sacrament of Writing: Robert Bresson's *Journal d'un curé de campagne*." In *French Film: Texts and Contexts*, edited by Susan Hayward and Ginette Vincendeau, 137–146. New York: Routledge, 1990.

Reed, Muriel. "Robert Bresson: Lens on the Soul." *Réalités* 87 (February 1958): 34–41.

Rohmer, Eric. "Le Miracle des objets." *Cahiers* 65 (December 1956): 42–45.

Ropars-Wuillemier, Marie-Claire. *De la littérature au cinéma: genèse d'une écriture*. Paris: Armand Colin, 1970.

Roud, Richard. "The Early Work of Robert Bresson." *Film Culture* 20 (1959): 44–52.

Richie, Donald. "Bresson and Music." In *Robert Bresson*, edited by James Quandt, 299–306. Toronto: Cinémathèque Ontario, 1998.

Robert Bresson: Éloge. Paris: Cinematèque française, 1997.

Rosenbaum, Jonathan. "The Last Filmmaker: A Local, Interim Report." In *Robert Bresson*, edited by James Quandt, 17–26. Toronto: Cinémathèque Ontario, 1998.

Roulet, Sébastien. "La si belle éthique de Robert Bresson." *Cahiers du cinéma* 189 (April 1967): 64–65.

————. "Les Rythmes d'un film doivent être des battements de cœur." *L'Express* 445 (December 1959): 38–39.

Sadoul, Georges. "Conversation plutôt qu'interview avec Robert Bresson sur *Mouchette*." *Les Lettres françaises* 1174 (March 1967): 18–19.

————. "Danse de mort." *Les Lettres françaises* 1174 (March 1967): 19–20.

————. "Robert Bresson: *Journal d'un curé de campagne*." *Les Lettres françaises* 542 (February 1951): 6.

Samuels, Charles Thomas. *Encountering Directors*. New York: Capricorn, 1972.

Schrader, Paul. "Robert Bresson, Possibly." *Film Comment* 13 (September 1977): 26–30.

————. *Transcendental Style in Film: Ozu, Bresson, Dreyer*. Los Angeles: University of California Press, 1972.

Sitney, P. Adams. "Cinematography vs. the Cinema: Bresson's Figures." In *Robert Bresson*, edited by James Quandt, 145–164. Toronto: Cinémathèque Ontario, 1998.

————. "The Rhetoric of Robert Bresson." In *Robert Bresson*, edited by James Quandt, 117–144. Toronto: Cinémathèque Ontario, 1998.

Sémolué, Jean. *Bresson ou l'acte pur des métamorphoses*. Paris: Flammarion, 1993.

————. "Les Personnages de Robert Bresson." *Cahiers du cinéma* 75 (October 1957): 10–15.

Sloane, Jane. *Robert Bresson: A Guide to References and Resources*. Boston: G.K. Hall, 1983.

Sontag, Susan. "Spiritual Style in the Films of Robert Bresson." In *Against Interpretation*. New York: Farrar, Straus and Giroux, 1966.

Susini, Marie. "Monsieur Bresson." *Le Nouvel Observateur* (March 1967): 42–43.

Tallenay, Jean-Louis. "Un cinéma enfin parlant." *Cahiers du cinéma* 9 (February 1953): 30–36.

Taylor, John Russel. *Cinema Eye, Cinema Ear: Some Key Filmmakers of the Sixties*. New York: Hill and Wang, 1964.

Tilliette, Xavier. "Les Films: *Mouchette* de Robert Bresson." *Études* (May 1967): 663–665.

Truffaut, François. "Une certaine tendance du cinéma français." *Cahiers du cinéma* 31 (January 1954): 15–28.

Zeman, Marvin. "The Suicide of Robert Bresson." *Cinema* 6 (Spring 1971): 37–42.

Critical Sources—General

Amengual, Barthélemy. *Clefs pour le cinéma*. Paris: Seghers, 1971.

Barthes, Roland. "Introduction à l'analyse structurale des récits." *Communications* 8 (1966): 1–27.

Bordwell, David. *Narration in the Fiction Film.* Madison: University of Wisconsin Press, 1985.

Genette, Gérard. "Discours du récit." In *Figures III.* Paris: Seuil, 1972.

Jost, François. *L'Œeil-caméra: entre film et roman.* Lyon: Presses Universitaires de Lyon, 1987.

Marie, Michel. *La Nouvelle Vague: une école artistique.* Paris: Nathan, 1997.

Metz, Christian. *Langage et cinéma.* Paris: Larousse, 1971.

Vanoye, Francis. *Récit écrit, récit filmique.* Paris: Éditions Nathan, 2002.

Currents in Comparative
Romance Languages and Literatures

This series was founded in 1987, and actively solicits book-length manuscripts (approximately 200–400 pages) that treat aspects of Romance languages and literatures. Originally established for works dealing with two or more Romance literatures, the series has broadened its horizons and now includes studies on themes within a single literature or between different literatures, civilizations, art, music, film and social movements, as well as comparative linguistics. Studies on individual writers with an influence on other literatures/civilizations are also welcome. We entertain a variety of approaches and formats, provided the scholarship and methodology are appropriate.

For additional information about the series or for the submission of manuscripts, please contact:

Tamara Alvarez-Detrell and Michael G. Paulson
c/o Dr. Heidi Burns
Peter Lang Publishing, Inc.
P.O. Box 1246
Bel Air, MD 21014-1246

To order other books in this series, please contact our Customer Service Department:

800-770-LANG (within the U.S.)
212-647-7706 (outside the U.S.)
212-647-7707 FAX

or browse online by series at:

www.peterlang.com